THE BODY

HOW IT WORKS

THE BODY

DR. KATE BARNES

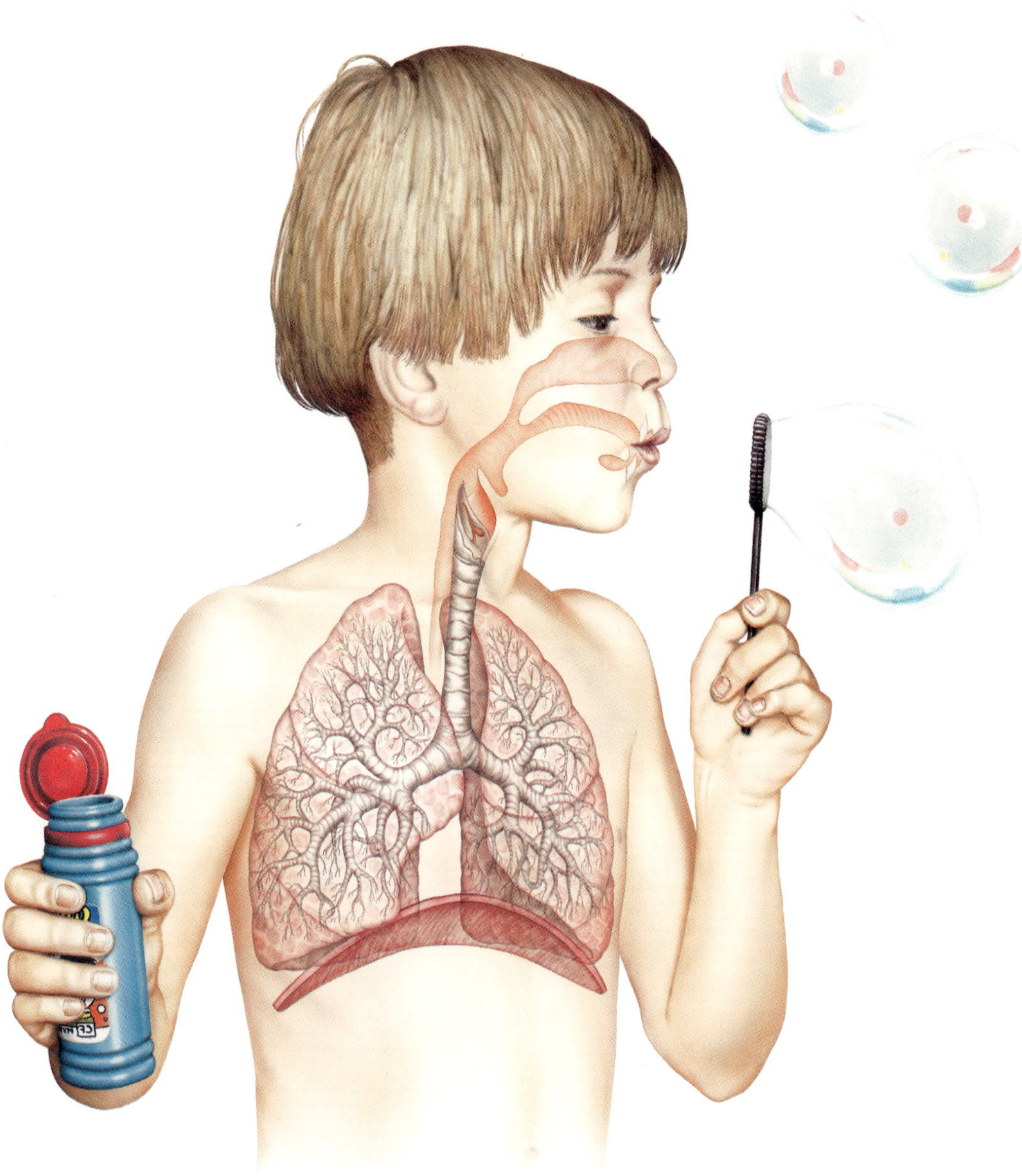

Cavendish Square

Published in 2025 by Cavendish Square Publishing, LLC
2544 Clinton Street, Buffalo, NY 14224

Website: cavendishsq.com

Series editor: Elizabeth Miles
Cover design: Duck Egg Blue
Illustrations: Steve Weston
Photography and additional illustrations: Shutterstock.com (Mikado767, RAJ CREATIONZS, Alex Mit, Life science, Samuel Borges Photography, vitstudio, Chaonucha Tipsoontornpong, Monkey Business Images, Zoltan Major, szefei, Oksana Kuzmina, vector illustration, Suzanne Tucker, Billion Photos, Romanova Natali, SciePro, PhawKStudio, Nenov Brothers Images, Igor Lateci, ShutterOK, canbedone, Romrodphoto, krutar, Rostislav_Sedlacek, MANDY GODBEHEAR, OndroM, Riccardo Mayer, Ladanifer); NASA

Cataloging-in-Publication Data

Names: Barnes, Kate.
Title: The body / Dr. Kate Barnes.
Description: Buffalo, NY : Cavendish Square Publishing, 2025. |
Series: How it works | Includes index.
Identifiers: ISBN 9781502671820 (pbk.) | ISBN 9781502671837 (library bound) |
ISBN 9781502671844 (ebook)
Subjects: LCSH: Human body--Juvenile literature.
Classification: LCC QP37.B736 2025 | DDC 612--dc23

CPSIA compliance information: Batch #CSCSQ25: For further information contact Cavendish Square Publishing LLC at 1-877-980-4450.

Printed in the United States of America

Find us on

Contents

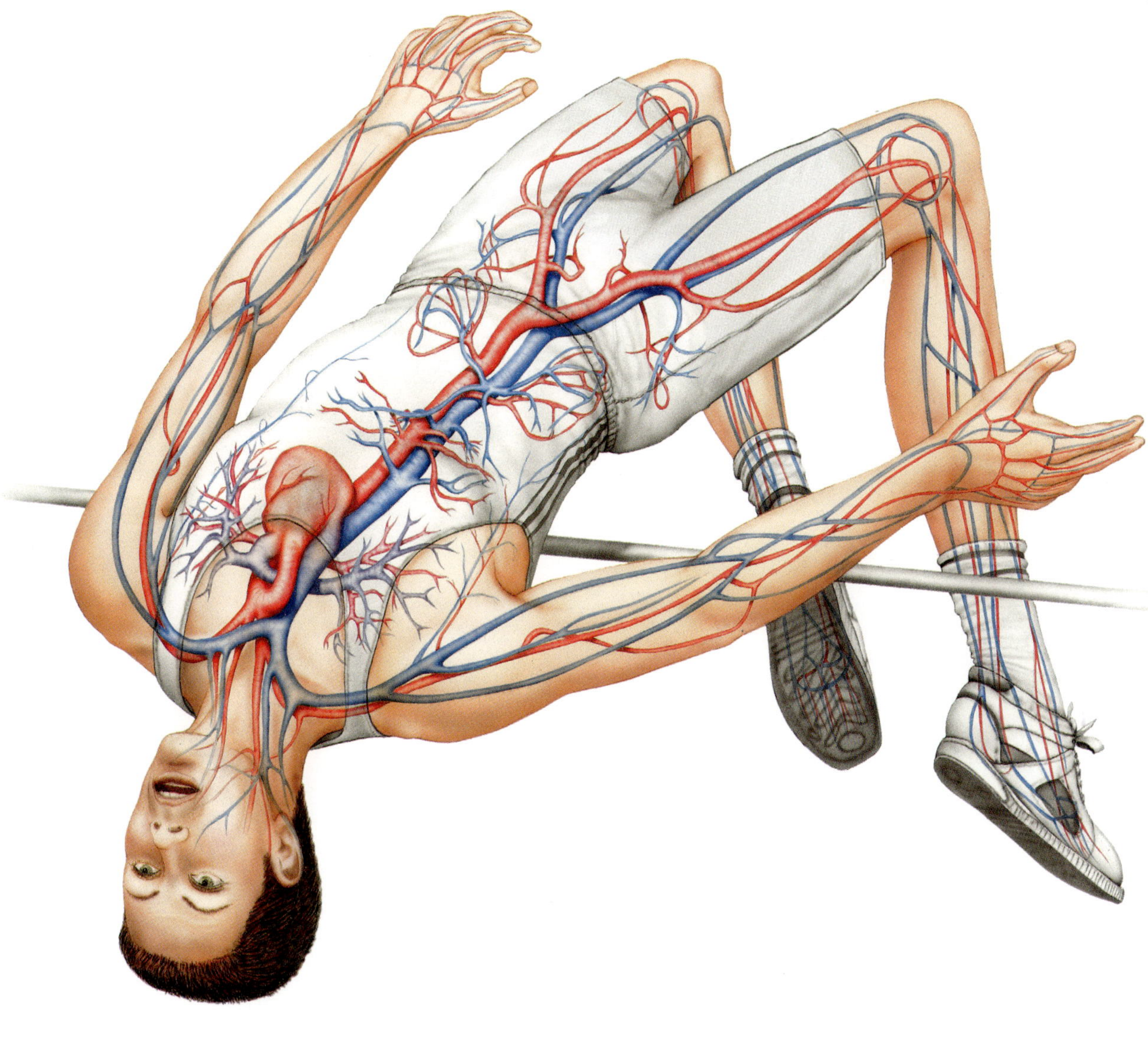

How the Body Works

Do you know what lies inside your body and how your body works? The following pages will take you on a voyage of discovery. Along the way, you will find out how each system in the body functions and how all the systems work together to make us the complex human beings we are.

In particular, you will see how each part of the body has its own special job to do, how we get the energy to live, and how we defend ourselves from harm. You will also learn about the five senses – vision, hearing, touch, taste, and smell – and how all we think and do is controlled by the brain in communication with our nervous system. This book explains how and why we breathe, how we move, and how we reproduce in order to keep the human race alive.

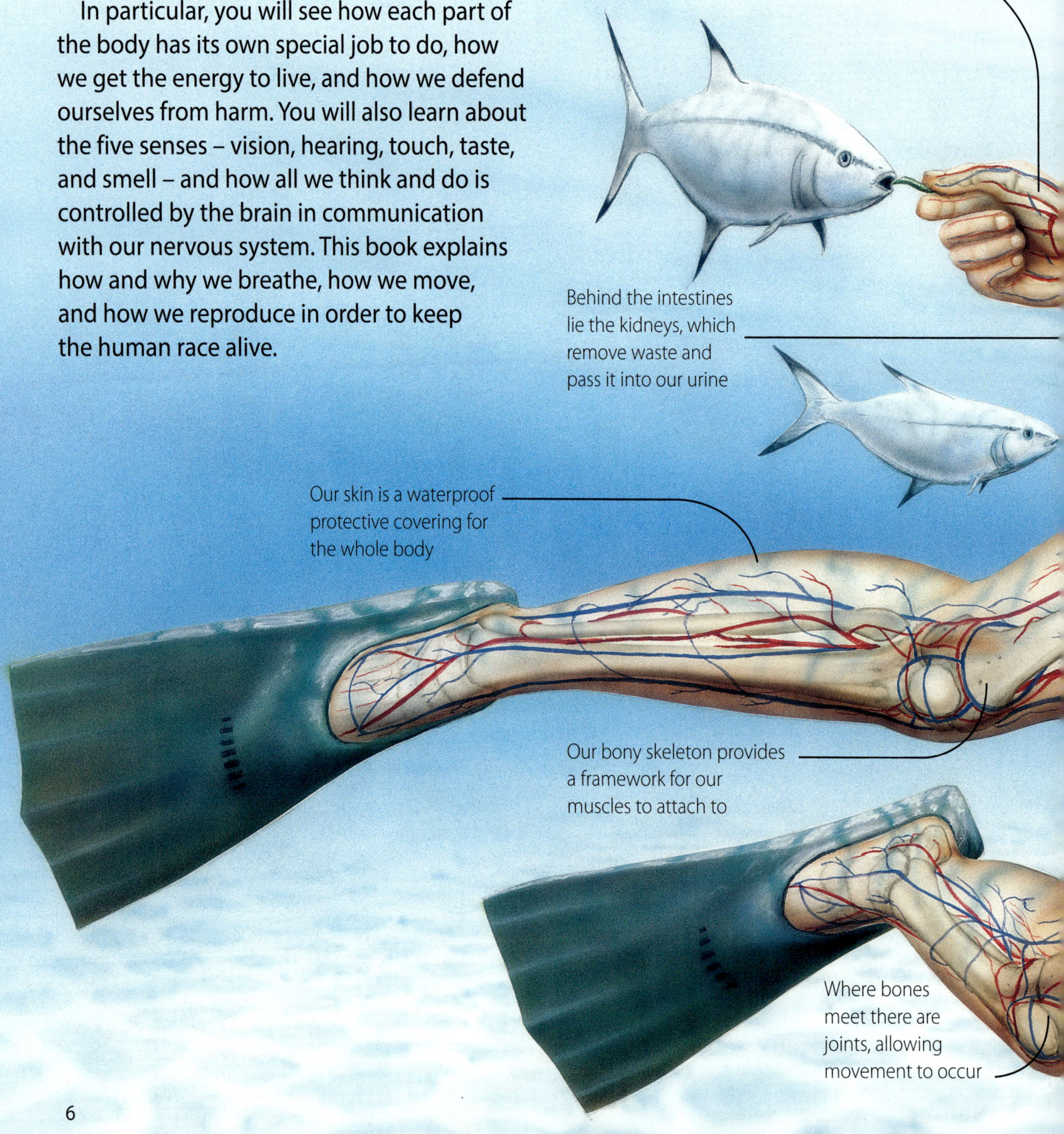

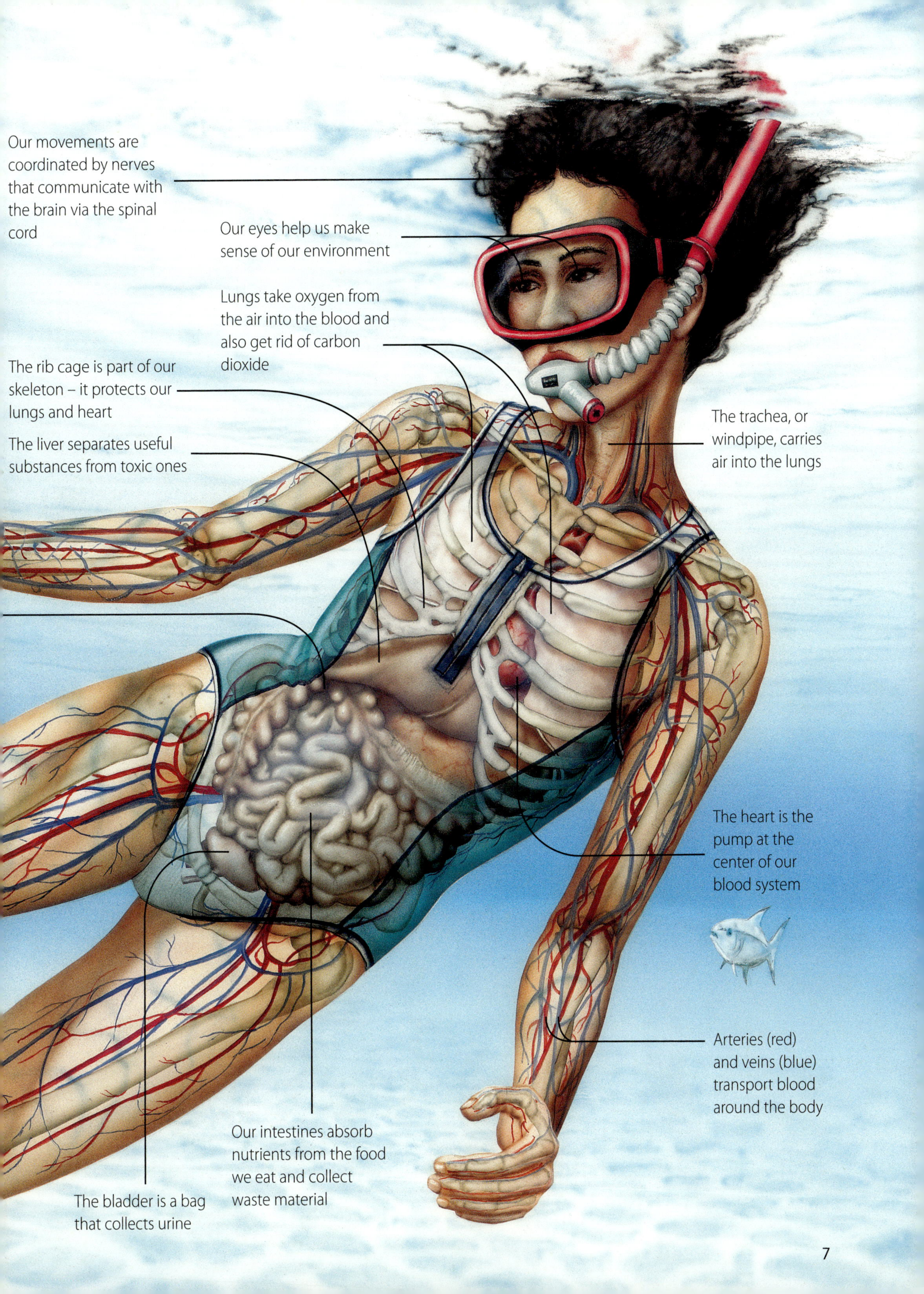
Our movements are coordinated by nerves that communicate with the brain via the spinal cord
Our eyes help us make sense of our environment
Lungs take oxygen from the air into the blood and also get rid of carbon dioxide
The rib cage is part of our skeleton – it protects our lungs and heart
The liver separates useful substances from toxic ones
The trachea, or windpipe, carries air into the lungs
The heart is the pump at the center of our blood system
Arteries (red) and veins (blue) transport blood around the body
Our intestines absorb nutrients from the food we eat and collect waste material
The bladder is a bag that collects urine

Cells

In total there are about 50 billion cells in your body! Each cell is so small that it cannot be seen with the naked eye. However, with the help of microscopes we are able to study cells and discover how they work.

Nearly all cells have a nucleus, which is the control center of the cell. Ribosomes in cells do as the nucleus tells them. They act like factories, making proteins and other chemicals for our body. To work properly, a cell needs energy, and this energy comes from the food we eat. Power stations in the cell, called mitochondria, change energy from food into energy that can be used by the cell.

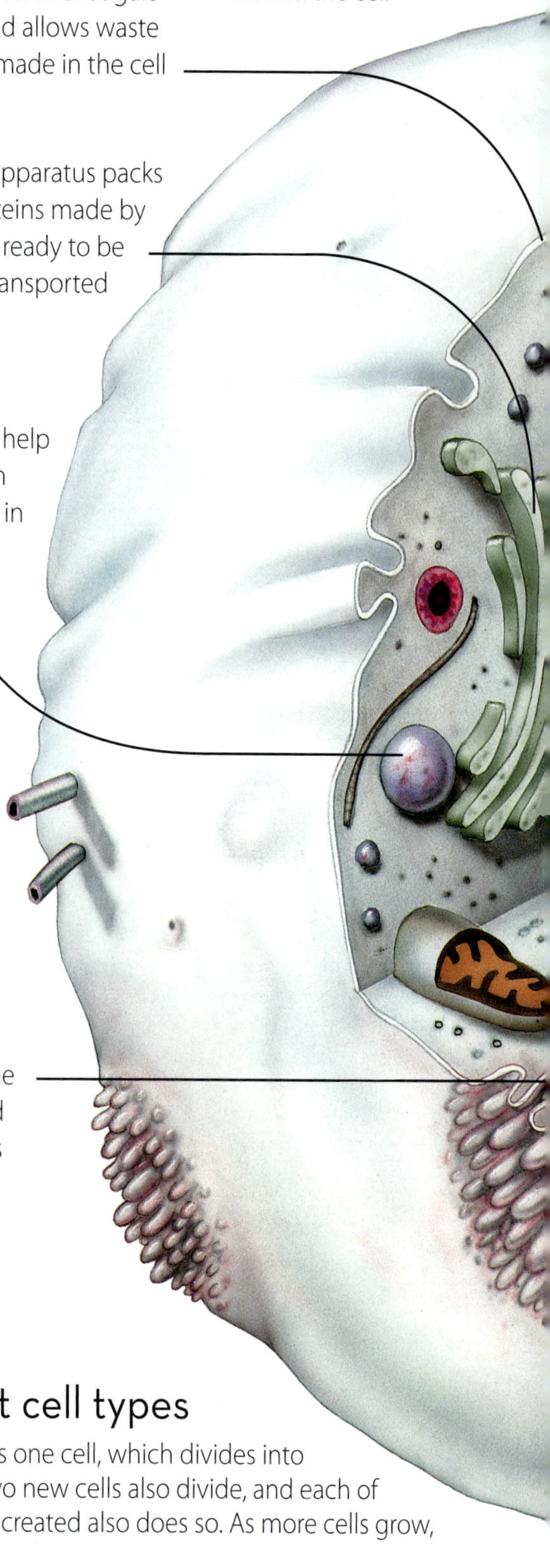

These branching tubes are used for storage and for transporting chemicals around the cell

The cell membrane allows food in the form of sugars to enter, and allows waste chemicals made in the cell to pass out

The Golgi apparatus packs up the proteins made by ribosomes, ready to be stored or transported

Lysosomes help break down substances in the cell

The control center of the cell is called the nucleus

Brain cells

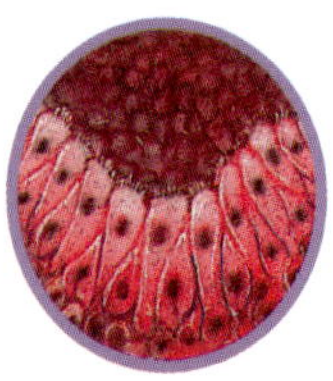

Lung cells

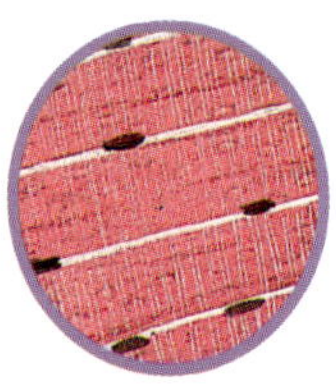

Muscle cells

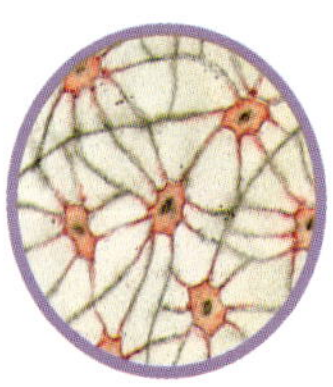

Bone cells

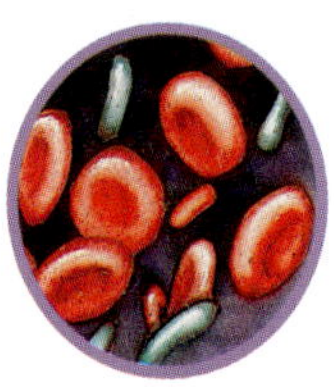

Blood cells

Different cell types

We start life as one cell, which divides into two. These two new cells also divide, and each of the new cells created also does so. As more cells grow, different types of cells begin to develop, each with its own job to do. Similar types of cells join together to make tissues that form organs such as our brain and lungs *(see left)*.

How long a cell lives depends on the type of cell it is. Skin cells are short-lived and are continuously replaced by new cells. Nerve cells should last a human lifetime and cannot be replaced even if they are damaged.

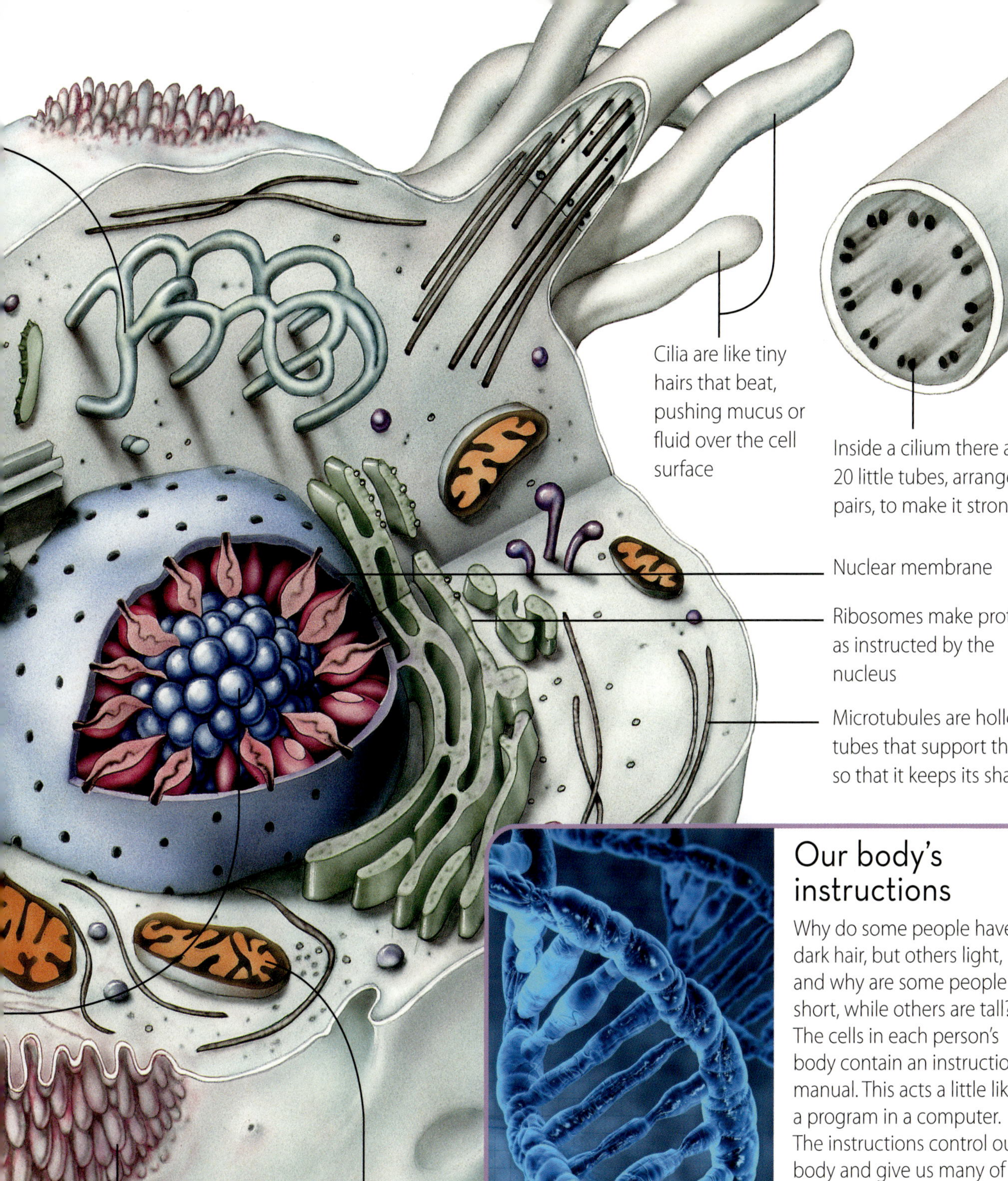

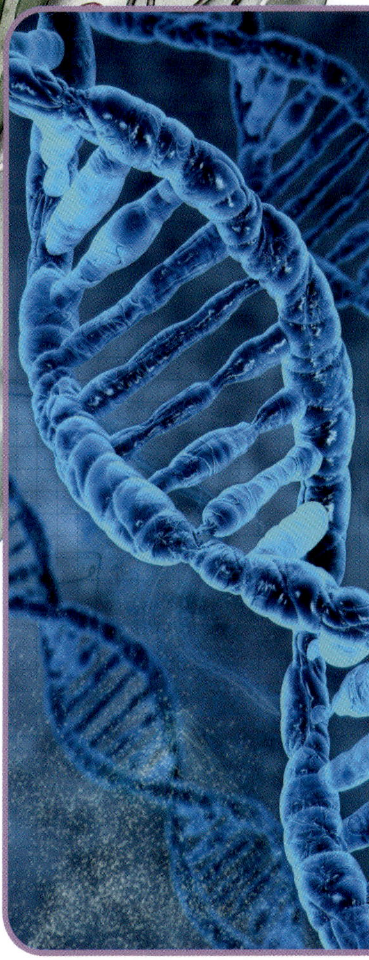

Our body's instructions

Why do some people have dark hair, but others light, and why are some people short, while others are tall? The cells in each person's body contain an instruction manual. This acts a little like a program in a computer. The instructions control our body and give us many of our characteristics.

Inside the nucleus of each cell are tiny threads called chromosomes. Inside the chromosomes are smaller structures called genes. It is in the genes that the instruction manual lies. The instructions are in the form of a chemical called DNA. DNA is shaped like a twisted ladder, known as a double helix.

The Blood System

Our blood acts as a transport system, carrying substances around the body. It is like a road network, with large arteries as main roads and very small blood vessels as lanes. Blood itself is made up of a liquid called plasma and two main types of cells – red cells and white cells. Red cells contain hemoglobin, which is responsible for carrying oxygen to the body's cells. White cells are far fewer in number than red cells. Their job is to attack invading germs. There are also small particles in blood called platelets, which help it to clot when we are injured and our skin is cut or grazed.

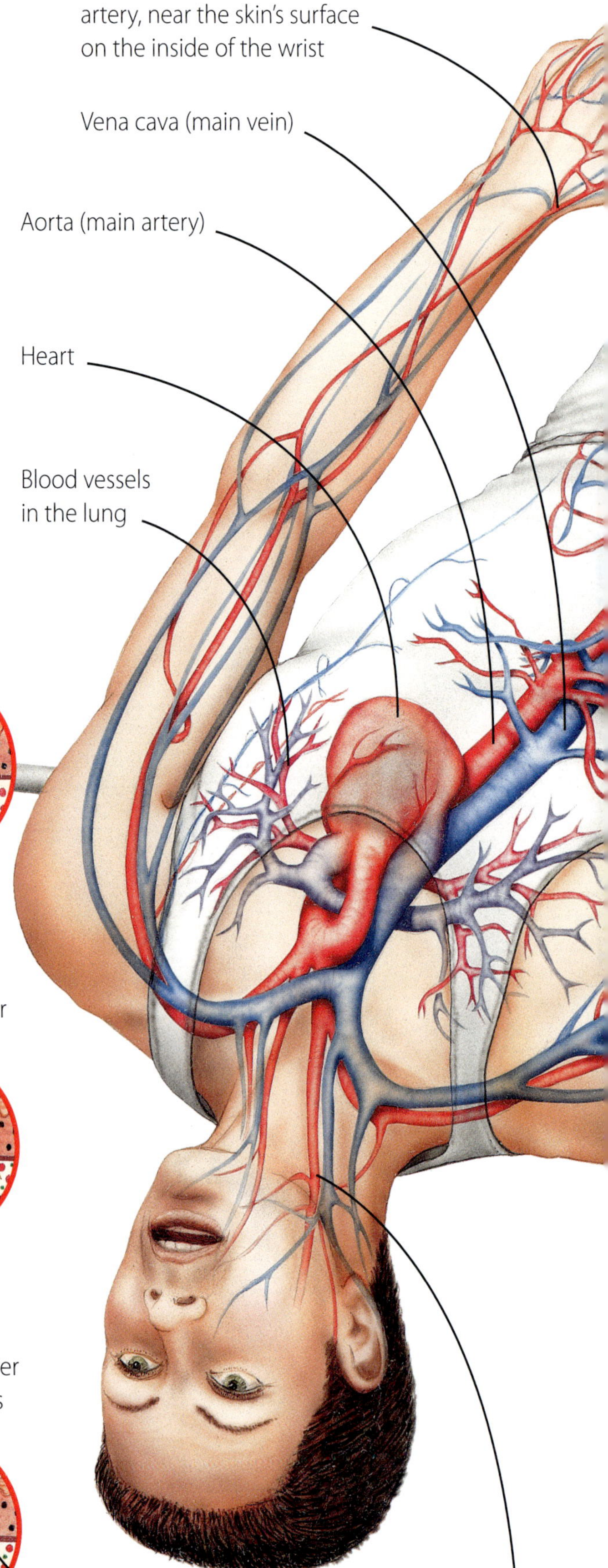

Forming a scab

Blood vessels lie beneath the skin, and if our skin is broken or cut, we usually bleed because the vessel walls break. The bleeding stops when enough platelets have stuck to the broken walls and signaled other substances to come. These substances form strands called fibrin, which form a web over the red blood cells to create a clot. A scab is the clot on the skin.

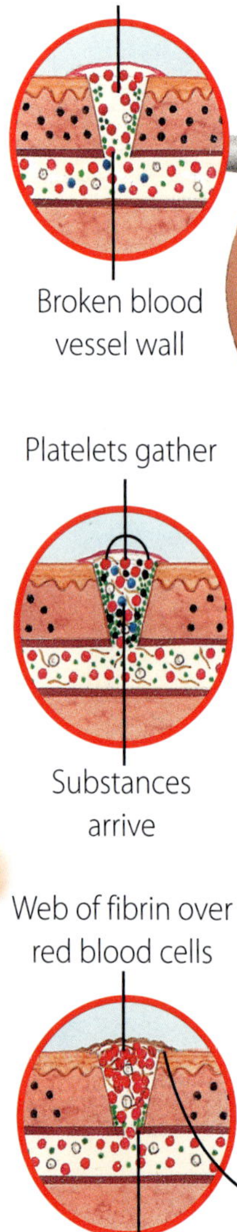

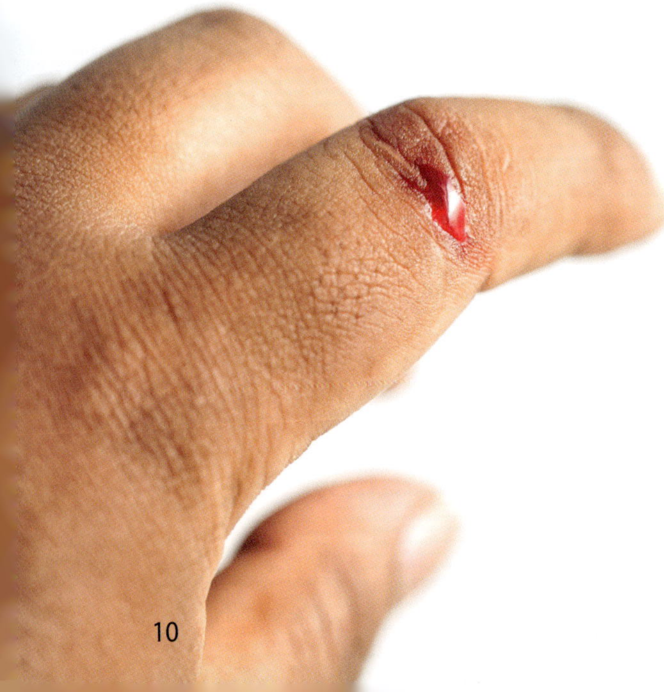

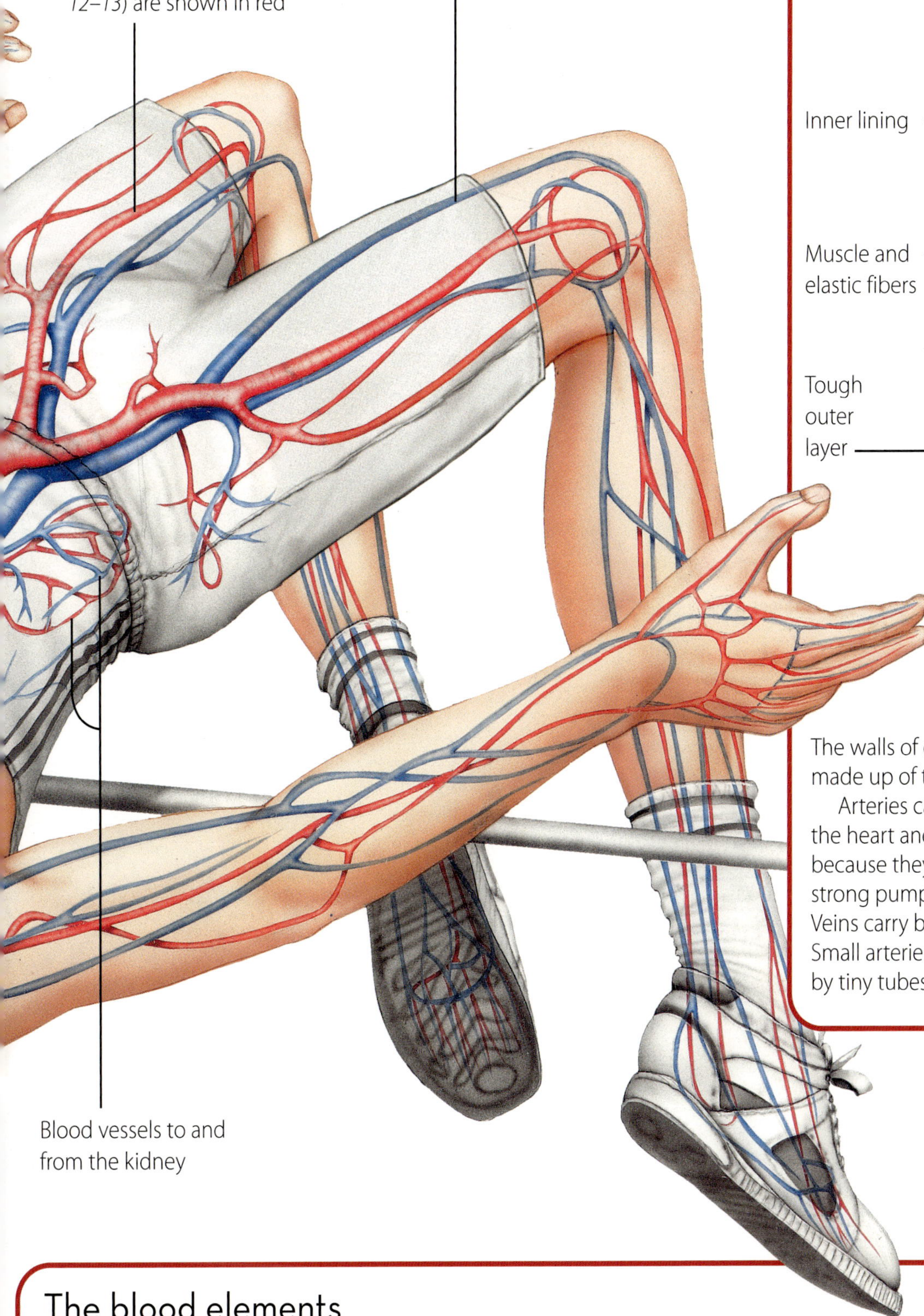

Blood vessels

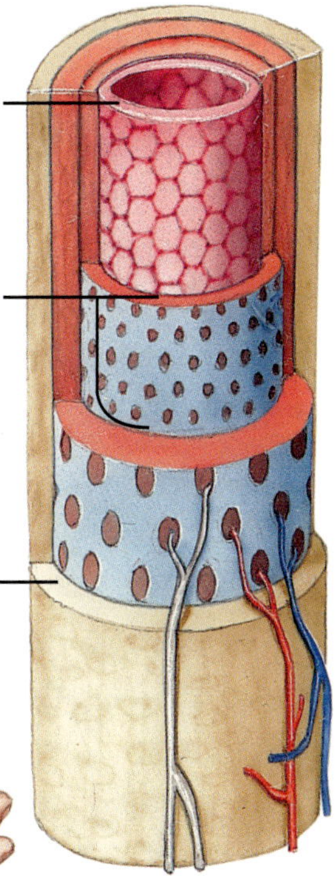

The walls of our arteries and veins are made up of three layers.

Arteries carry blood away from the heart and are thicker than veins because they must withstand the strong pumping action of the heart. Veins carry blood back to the heart. Small arteries and veins are linked by tiny tubes called capillaries.

The blood elements

Pictured here are the main blood elements as seen through a microscope.

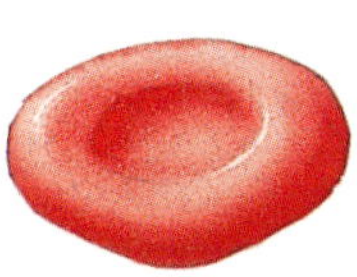
A red blood cell – also called an erythrocyte

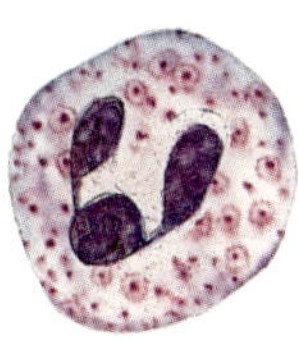
A common white cell

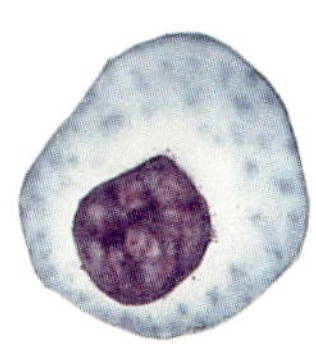
Another type of white cell – it forms antibodies

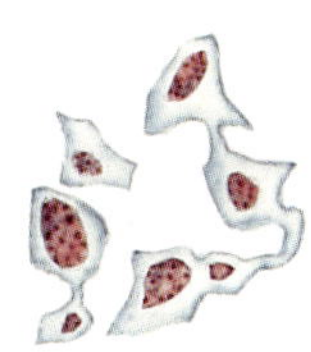
Platelets – sticky particles

The Heart

Our heart is the pump at the center of our blood – or circulatory – system. Heart muscle is very strong, as it has to pump blood through the networks of blood vessels around the body. Heart muscle contracts automatically; the number of times it contracts, or beats, in a minute is known as the heart rate. An adult normally has a heart rate of between 60 and 100 beats a minute. At birth, our heart rate is much faster than this – sometimes twice as fast. A child's heart rate is usually faster than an adult's but gradually slows until they are around 10 years old. Everyone's normal heart rate increases when they exercise because more oxygen, carried by the blood, is needed by hardworking muscles.

You can measure your heart rate by feeling your pulse. Your wrist is one place that you can find it. If you put two fingers across the underside of your wrist, where the artery lies close to the surface of your skin, you can count the number of beats felt in one minute.

Inside the heart

The heart is made up of four sections, called chambers. These chambers are the right and left atria, and the right and left ventricles. The ventricles are separated from the atria by valves, which are like one-way swing doors. Valves ensure that blood flows through the chambers in the right direction.

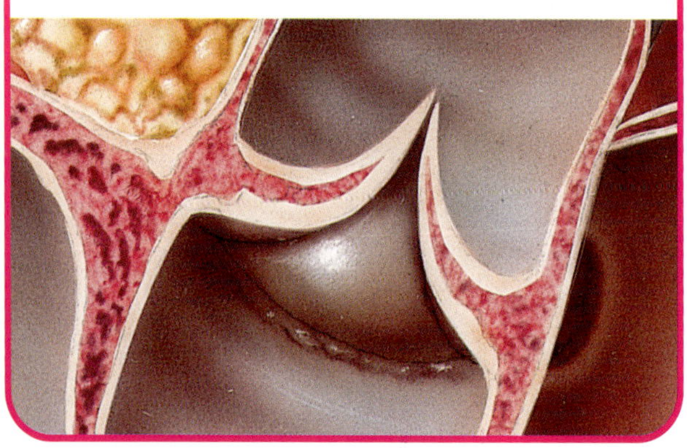

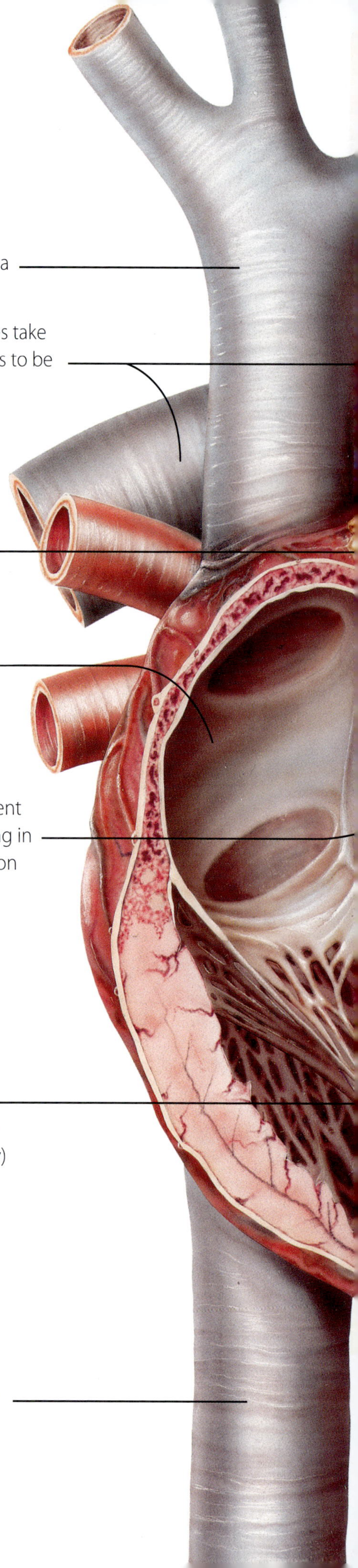

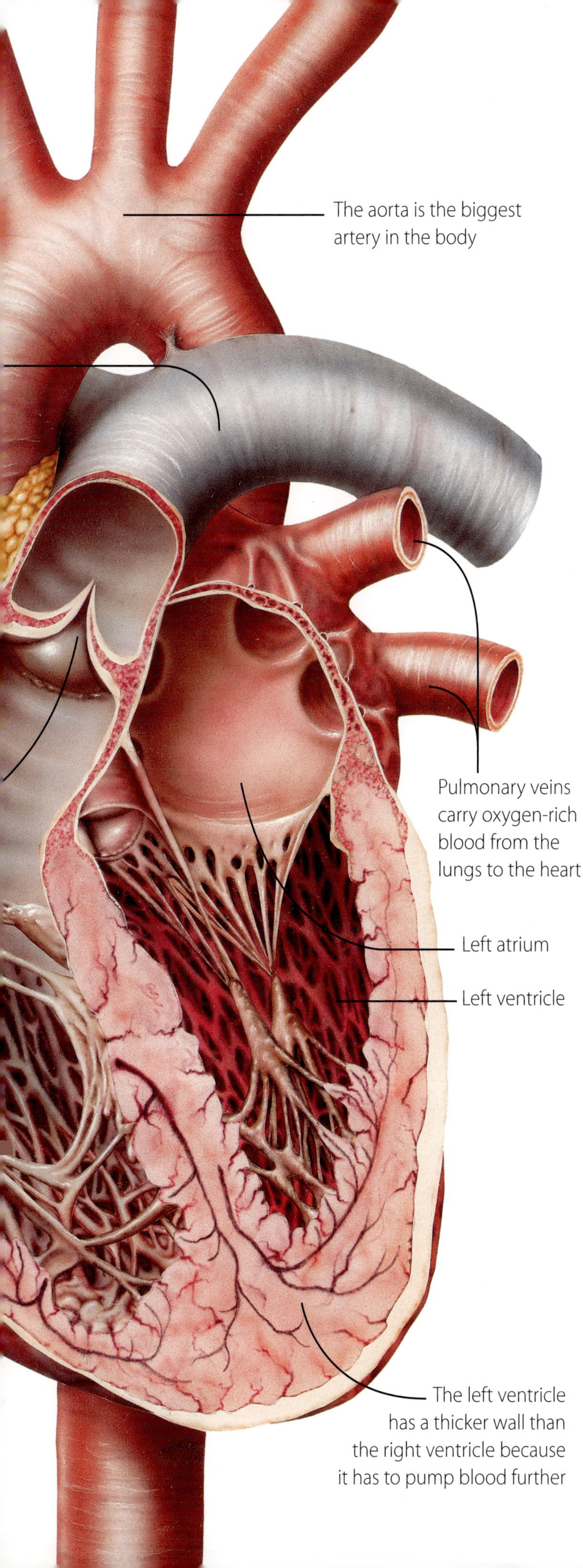

The flow of blood

The diagrams below show the direction that blood flows through the heart. The pulmonary veins carry blood rich in oxygen from the lungs to the left atrium (1). The blood then flows through the left ventricle (2) into the aorta (3). After this, it is pumped around the body. At the same time that newly oxygenated blood leaves the heart, more blood arrives at the right atrium through the large vein called the vena cava (1). This blood contains little oxygen because it has already been used by the body. Blood flows to the right ventricle (2) and then into the pulmonary artery to pick up more oxygen in the lungs (3). This cycle then repeats (4).

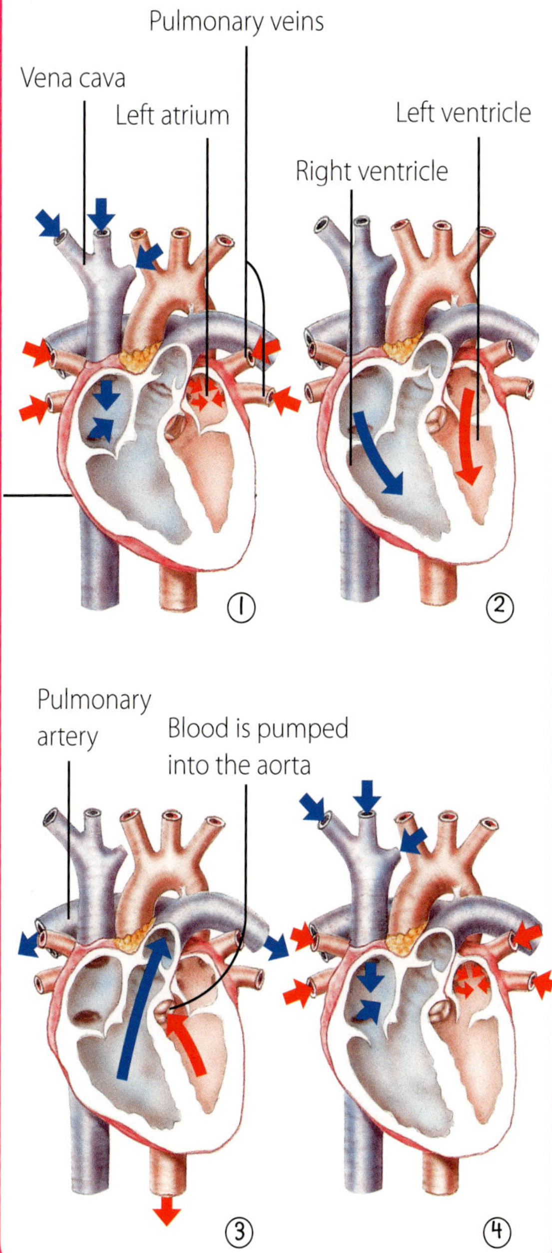

Breathing

Every time you breathe, you draw in air containing a gas called oxygen, which makes your body work. Most adults breathe 18 times a minute – children breathe faster. When you breathe in, hairs in your nose and mucus in your nose and throat help to prevent harmful particles of dust and bacteria from entering your lungs. The air travels down the trachea (windpipe) and into your lungs through the left and right bronchi. Your ribs move outward and your diaphragm muscle moves down, allowing your lungs to expand and fill with air. The opposite happens when you breathe out.

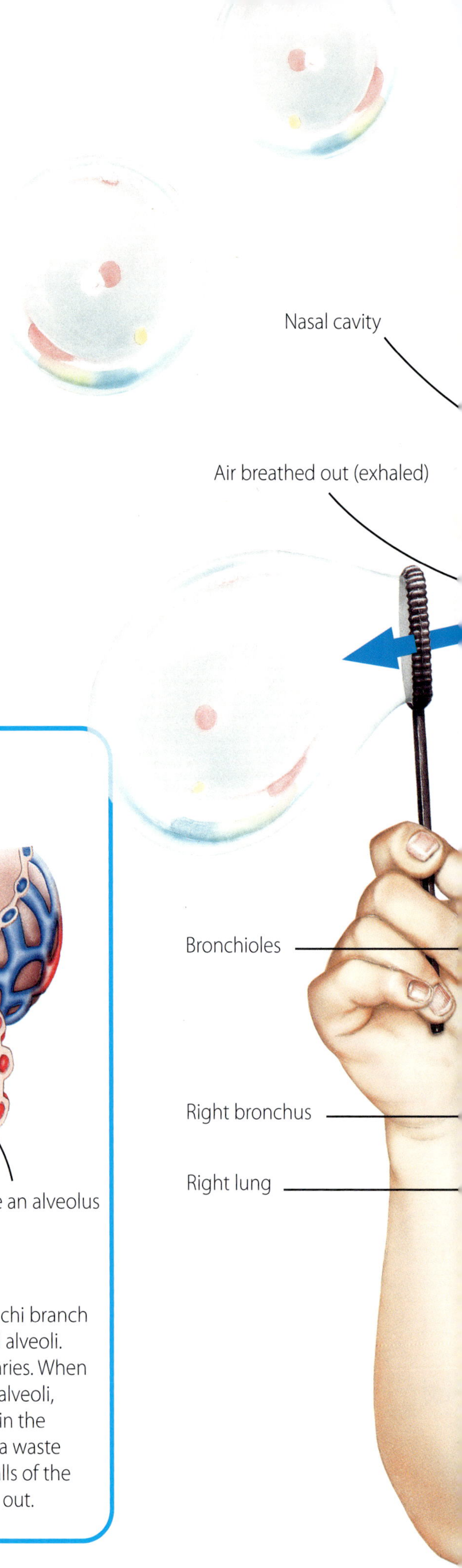

How oxygen passes into the bloodstream

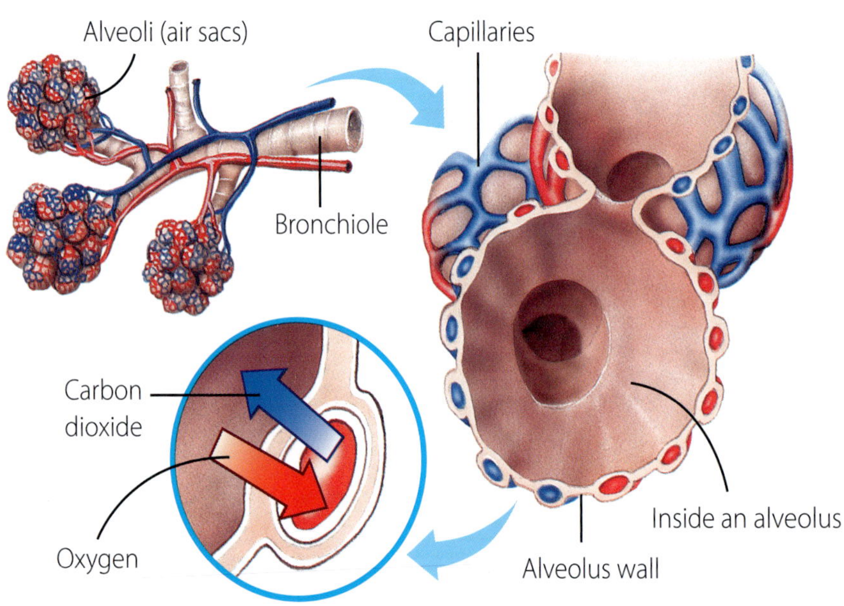

The inside of a lung looks like a large sponge. The left and right bronchi branch into thousands of small bronchioles, which end in tiny air sacs called alveoli. These alveoli are surrounded by very fine blood vessels called capillaries. When we breathe in, the oxygen in the air passes through the walls of the alveoli, which are thinner than tissue paper, into the capillaries. The oxygen in the blood is then transported to cells around the body. Carbon dioxide, a waste gas, is transported in the opposite direction, from the cells to the walls of the alveoli. We get rid of carbon dioxide in our bodies when we breathe out.

When we run around or exercise, the muscles in our bodies work harder, our bodies use more oxygen, and we produce more carbon dioxide.

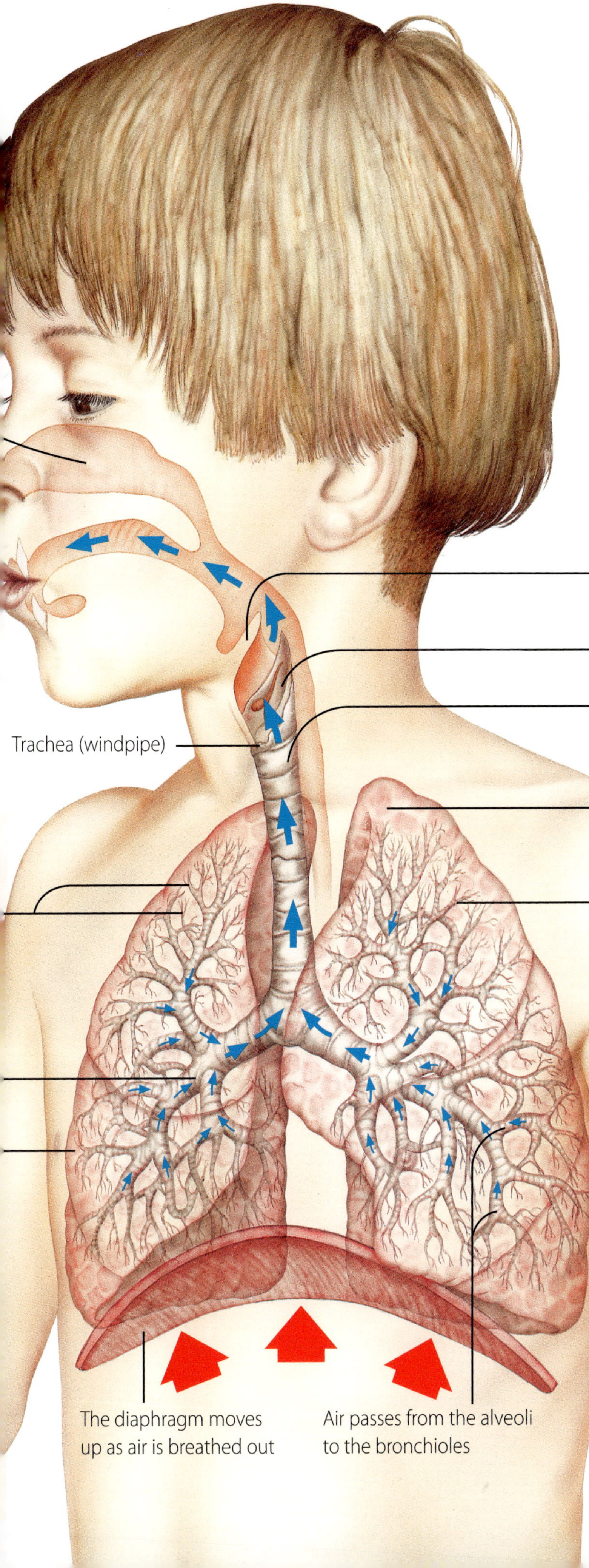
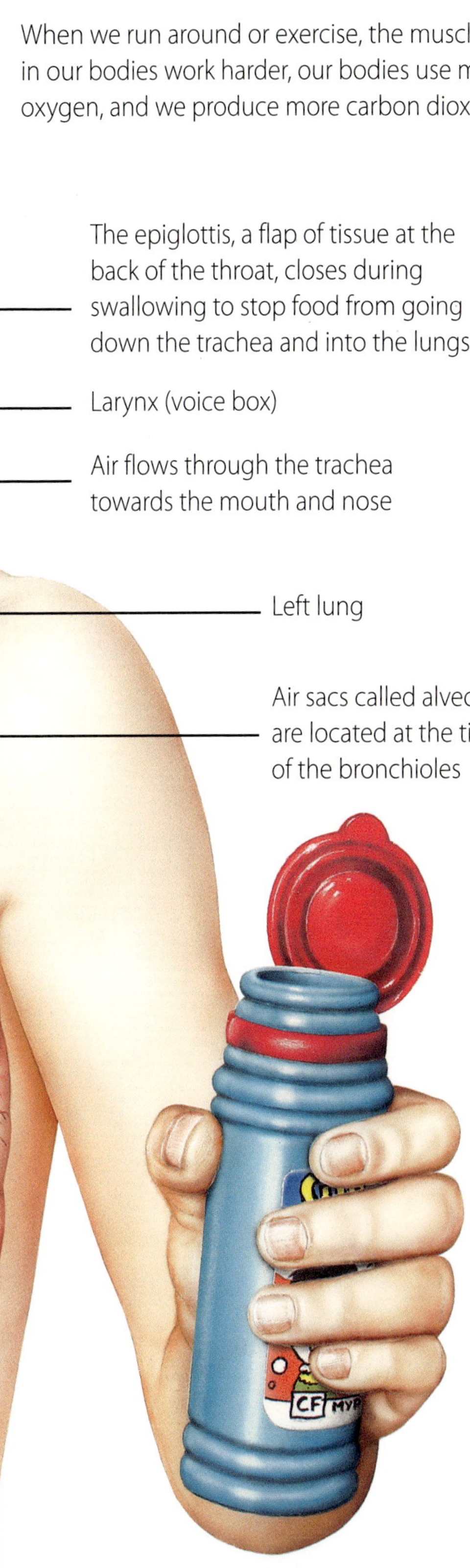

The Skeleton

The human skeleton is made up of more than 200 bones, which vary in shape and size to suit their function. The skeleton gives our muscles a firm place to anchor themselves and also protects our body's more fragile organs. For example, the brain is protected by the skull and the lungs are protected by the ribs. The spine, or backbone, is made up of 33 separate bones. It is shaped to protect the spinal cord, which travels through it, while also giving the spinal muscles a place for attachment.

The male skeleton is different from the female skeleton – the pelvis of a female skeleton is lower and wider than the male's. This helps women to carry a baby during pregnancy, and to deliver it safely during childbirth.

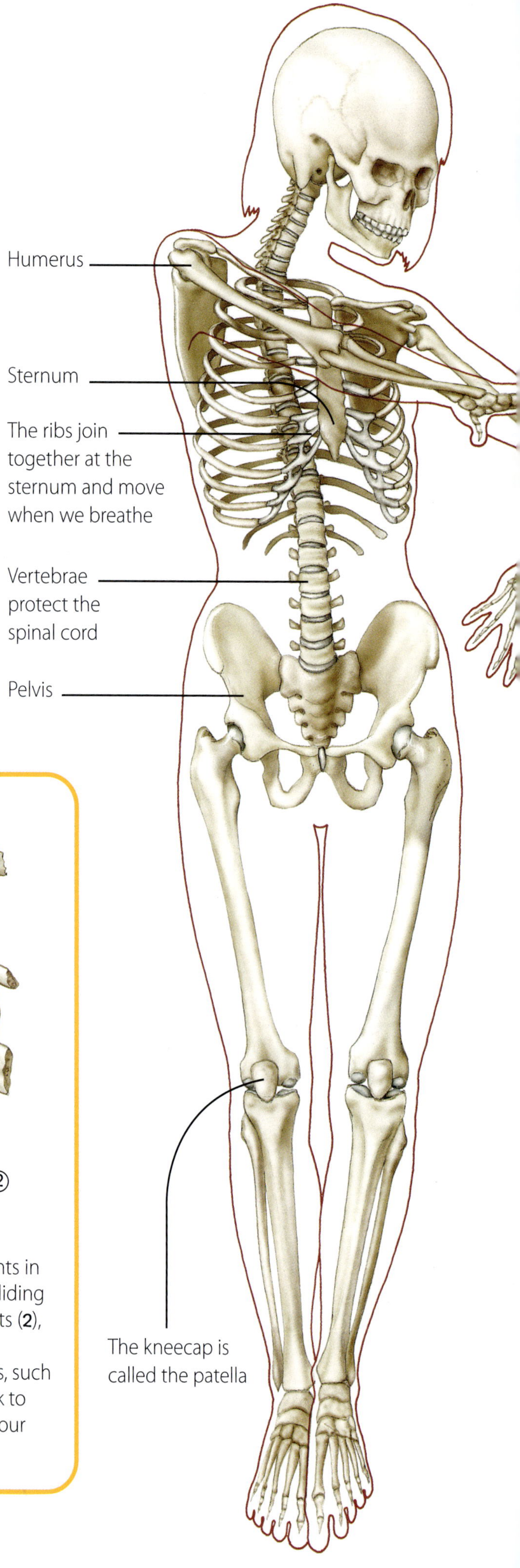

Joints

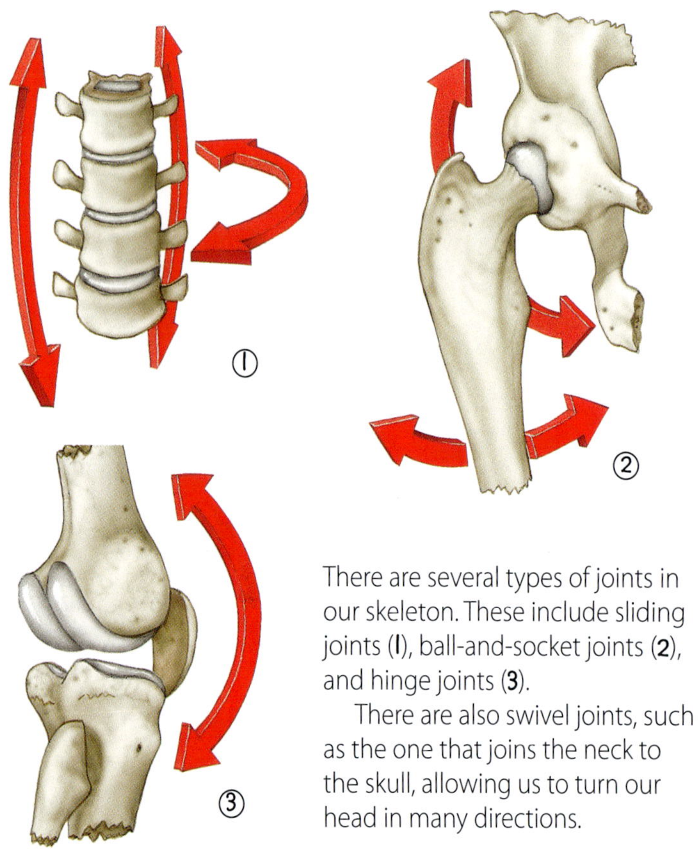

There are several types of joints in our skeleton. These include sliding joints (**1**), ball-and-socket joints (**2**), and hinge joints (**3**).

There are also swivel joints, such as the one that joins the neck to the skull, allowing us to turn our head in many directions.

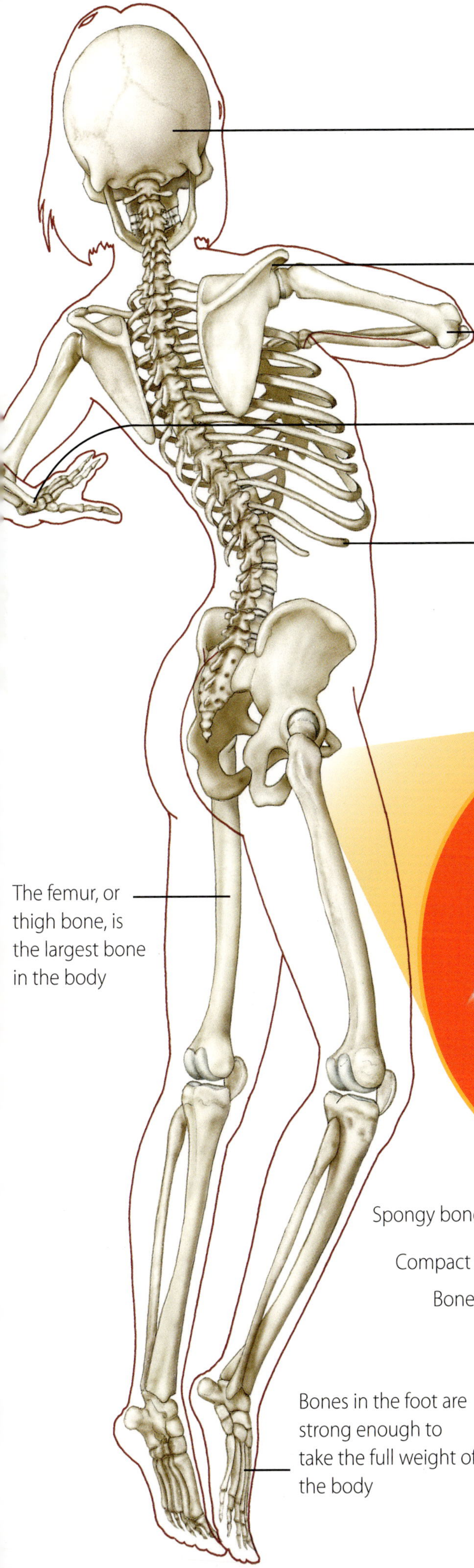

Inside a bone

Bones have an outer layer called the periosteum. This contains nerves and blood vessels. Underneath lies the toughest part – compact bone. This part is hollow and is lined with spongy bone, which makes it strong but not too heavy. Cells in the bone take calcium and phosphorus from the blood to keep the bony substance hard. Bone marrow lies at the center of bone. The bone marrow at the end of long bones is responsible for making new blood cells.

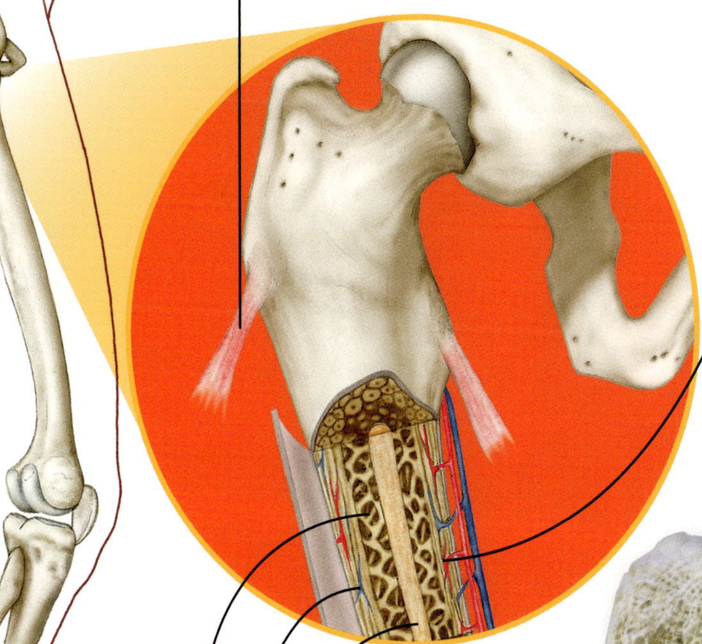

This photo (*right*) shows a cross-section of a human bone. You can see the knitted, fibrous texture that makes up the inside of the bone.

Muscles

We have lots of muscles of different shapes and sizes, ranging from the large gluteus maximus, on which we sit, to the tiny muscles that control the movements of our eyes. Many of our movements – when riding a bicycle, for example – involve a number of muscles that have to work together, and these are controlled by the brain. Every muscle in our body is made up of muscle fibers. Messages from the brain can make muscle fibers contract, making them shorter. As they shorten, they pull on the bones to which they are attached. This causes movement.

Automatic muscles

Although we can control many of our muscles, we also have muscles in our body that work automatically. These include the muscles that make our heart beat and the muscles in our intestines that help us to digest food.

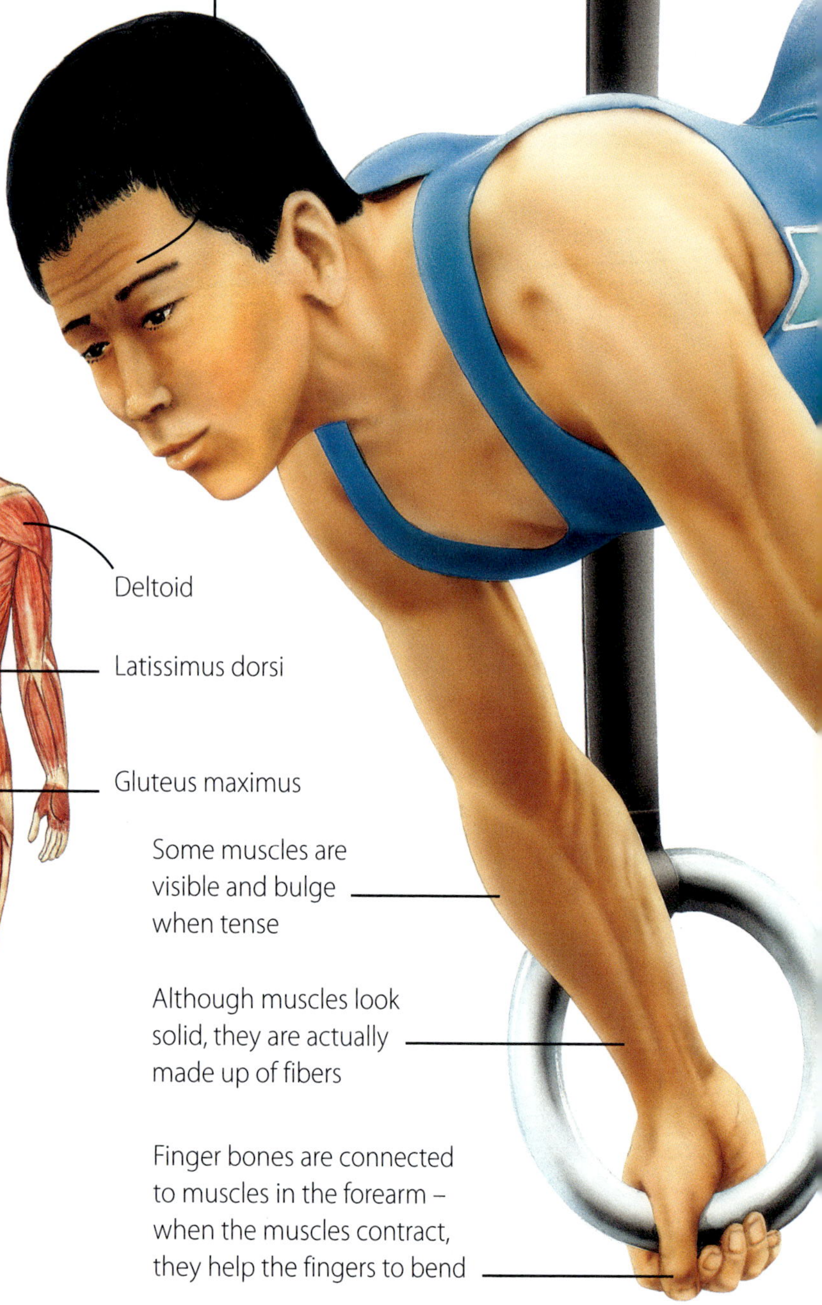

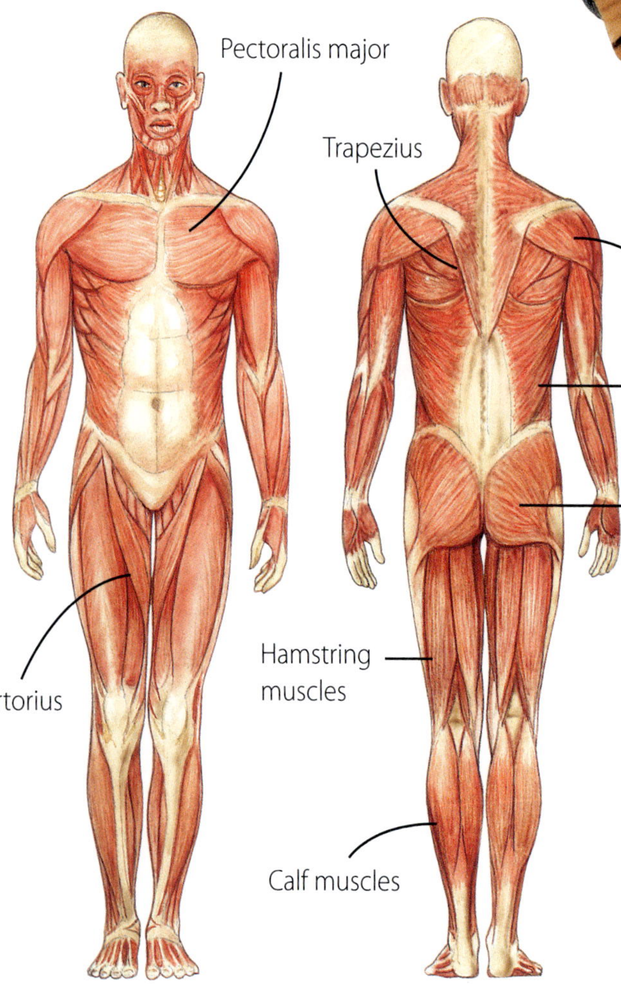

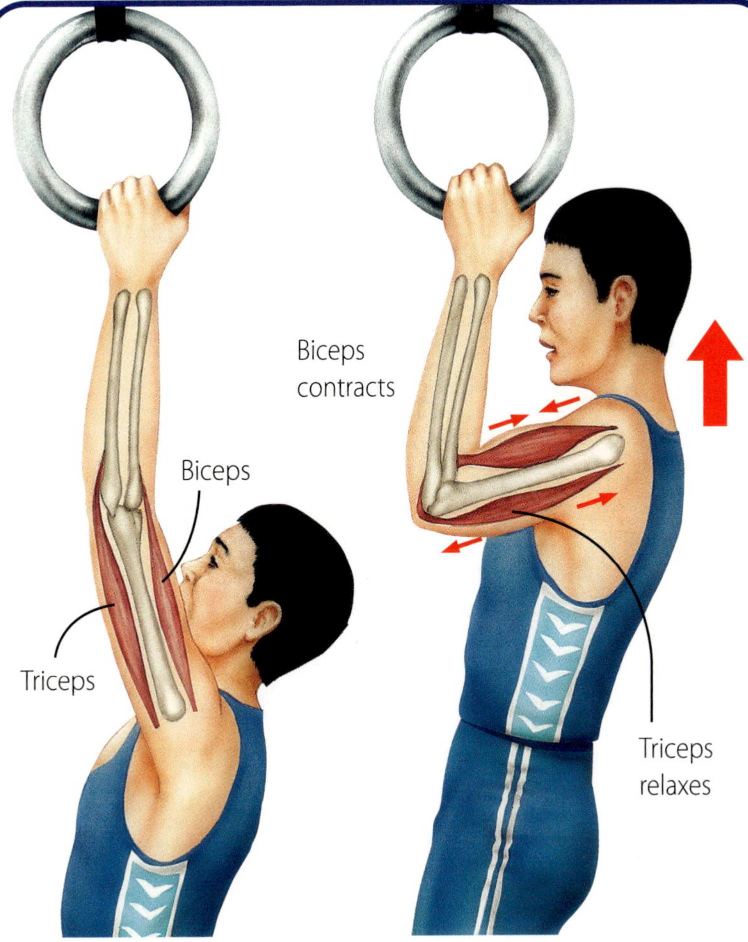

Muscle-building

Muscles often work in pairs. We can see this when a gymnast does a pull-up. Their biceps muscles shorten and stiffen, while their triceps muscles lengthen and relax. Regular training and frequent use of these muscles will increase their size and strength. This explains why many athletes have muscles you can easily see.

Flexibility

Without muscles, the body could not move. Some people have more flexibility than others, meaning they can bend and stretch their muscles more than other people.

We can all improve our flexibility by doing careful stretches regularly.

The Digestive System

We need food in order to live – it is the fuel for our body's energy and growth. There are three main kinds of food: protein (found in meat, cheese, and nuts, for example), carbohydrates (found in bread and potatoes), and fat (found in oils and butter). Proteins are used for repairing the body and for growing; carbohydrates and fats are needed to provide energy.

Digestion is a process that begins when we put food in our mouths and ends when the food has been absorbed into the bloodstream. It takes up to 18 hours for digestion to occur. This is not surprising because our food has to travel through about 26 feet (8 m) of coiled-up tubing, called the small intestine. On its journey, food gets broken down by acid and enzymes. An enzyme is a chemical that changes food into a substance we can easily absorb.

Small or large

Even though the small intestine is longer than the large intestine, it is called small because the diameter of the tube is narrower than that of the large intestine.

Food's journey

When we chew, our teeth break up food into small pieces for swallowing. Food then travels down a muscular tube, called the esophagus, to the stomach, which is a bag containing acid that kills off any bacteria (**1**). Next, food enters the small intestine (**2**). There, it is broken down into useful substances and waste materials by enzymes, which are produced by a gland called the pancreas.

Inside the small intestine, fingerlike bumps, known as villi, contain blood vessels that absorb the useful substances into the bloodstream. Waste substances remain and pass into the large intestine, where water is absorbed until the waste becomes solid (**3**). The waste is later expelled through the rectum.

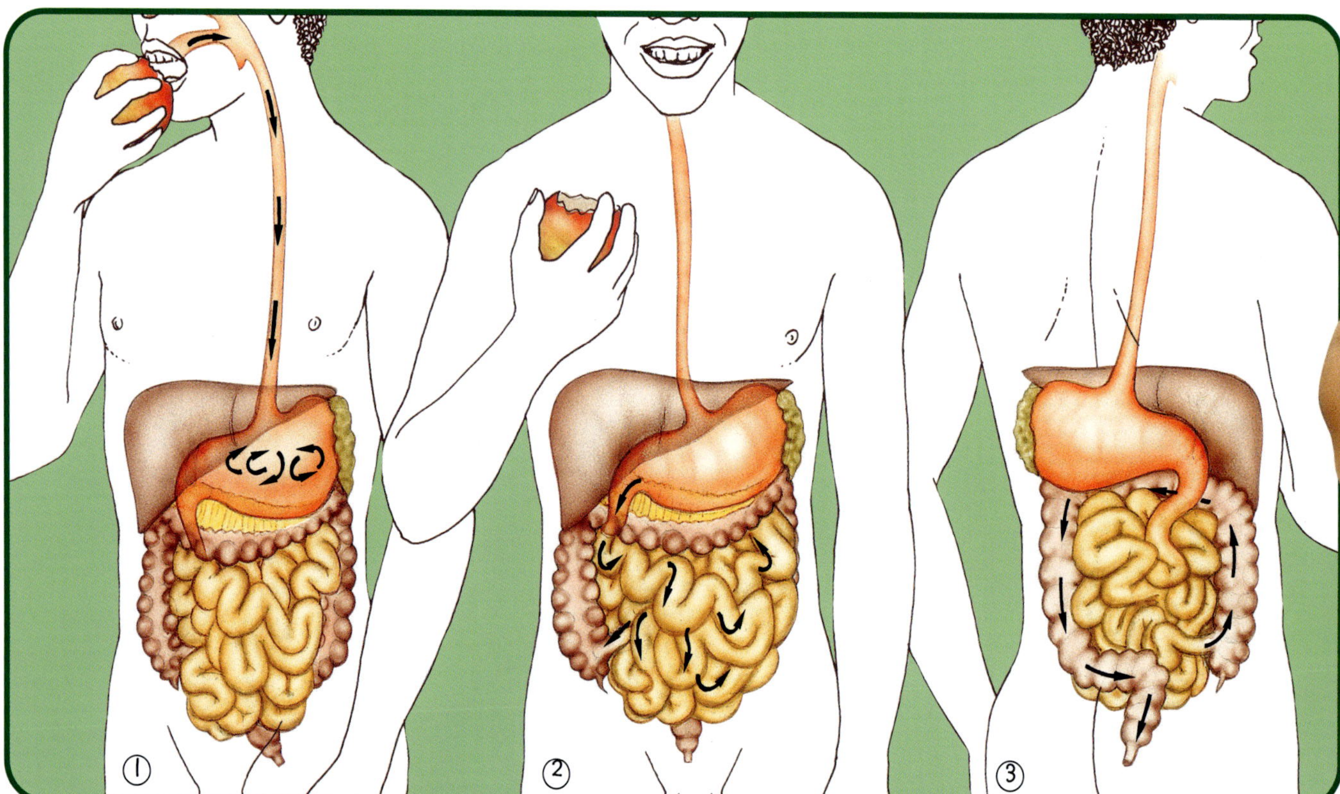

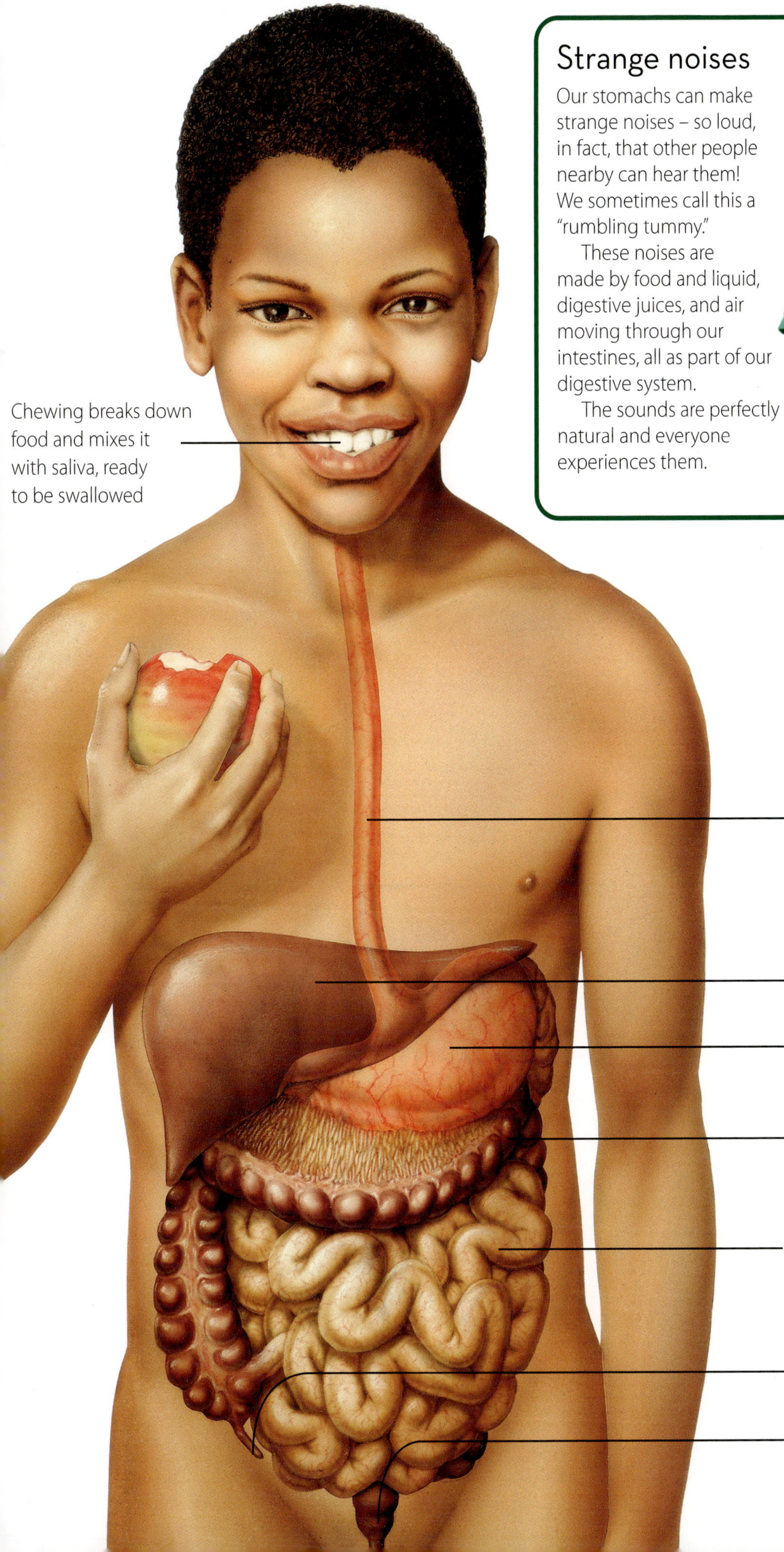

Strange noises

Our stomachs can make strange noises – so loud, in fact, that other people nearby can hear them! We sometimes call this a "rumbling tummy."

These noises are made by food and liquid, digestive juices, and air moving through our intestines, all as part of our digestive system.

The sounds are perfectly natural and everyone experiences them.

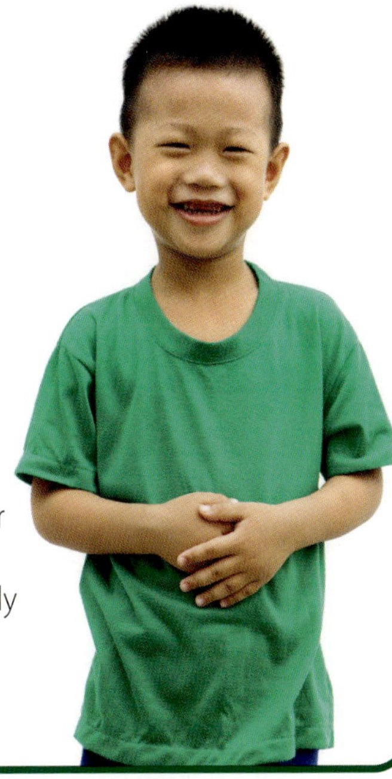

Teeth

Teeth begin the digestion process by breaking down food into small pieces for swallowing. The teeth at the front of the mouth, called incisors, are used for cutting. Behind these are the canine teeth, which are especially good for tearing tough food. The flatter teeth at the back are called premolars and molars – they are used for grinding and mashing.

Our first set of teeth, known as "milk teeth," appear in infancy. One of the lower incisors is usually the first tooth that comes through, at about seven months of age. The upper teeth appear soon after and the premolars emerge around our first birthday. From around six years of age, a second set of teeth grows, replacing our milk teeth. These teeth are complete when the "wisdom teeth," which are molars at the very back of the mouth, come through at around the age of 20. In total, an adult has 32 teeth.

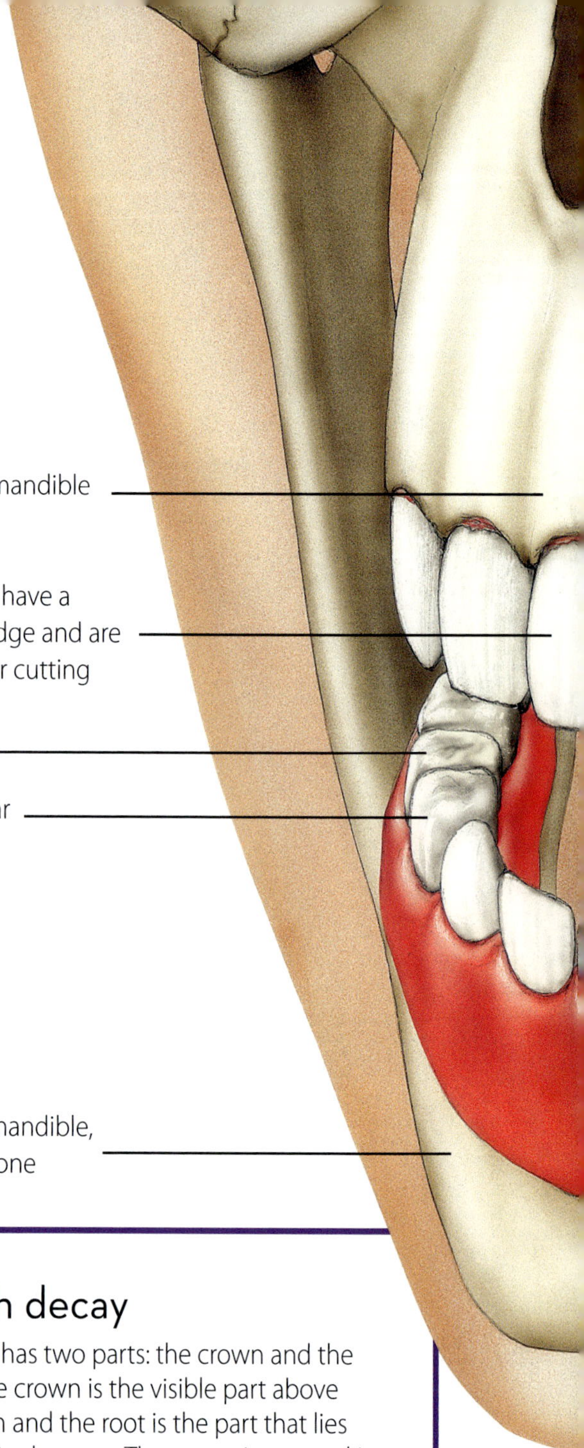

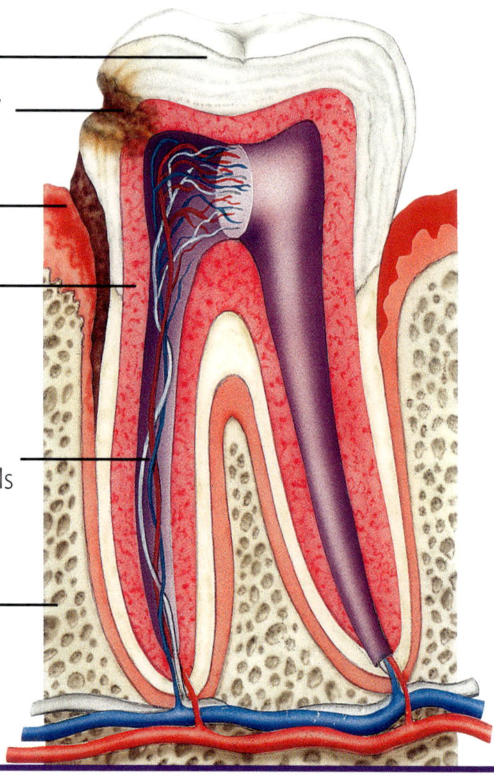

Tooth decay

A tooth has two parts: the crown and the root. The crown is the visible part above the gum and the root is the part that lies hidden in the gum. The crown is covered in enamel – the hardest substance in the body – which helps to protect the fragile blood vessels and nerves that lie inside the tooth. Dentine, another hard layer, surrounds and protects the center of the tooth. If our teeth are not cleaned regularly, sugar and bacteria in our mouths can make our teeth rot. This is because together they cause the production of acid, which breaks down enamel and causes dental decay.

Our gums can also become infected and begin to bleed. Brushing our teeth twice a day removes the sugar and bacteria and helps to stop tooth decay.

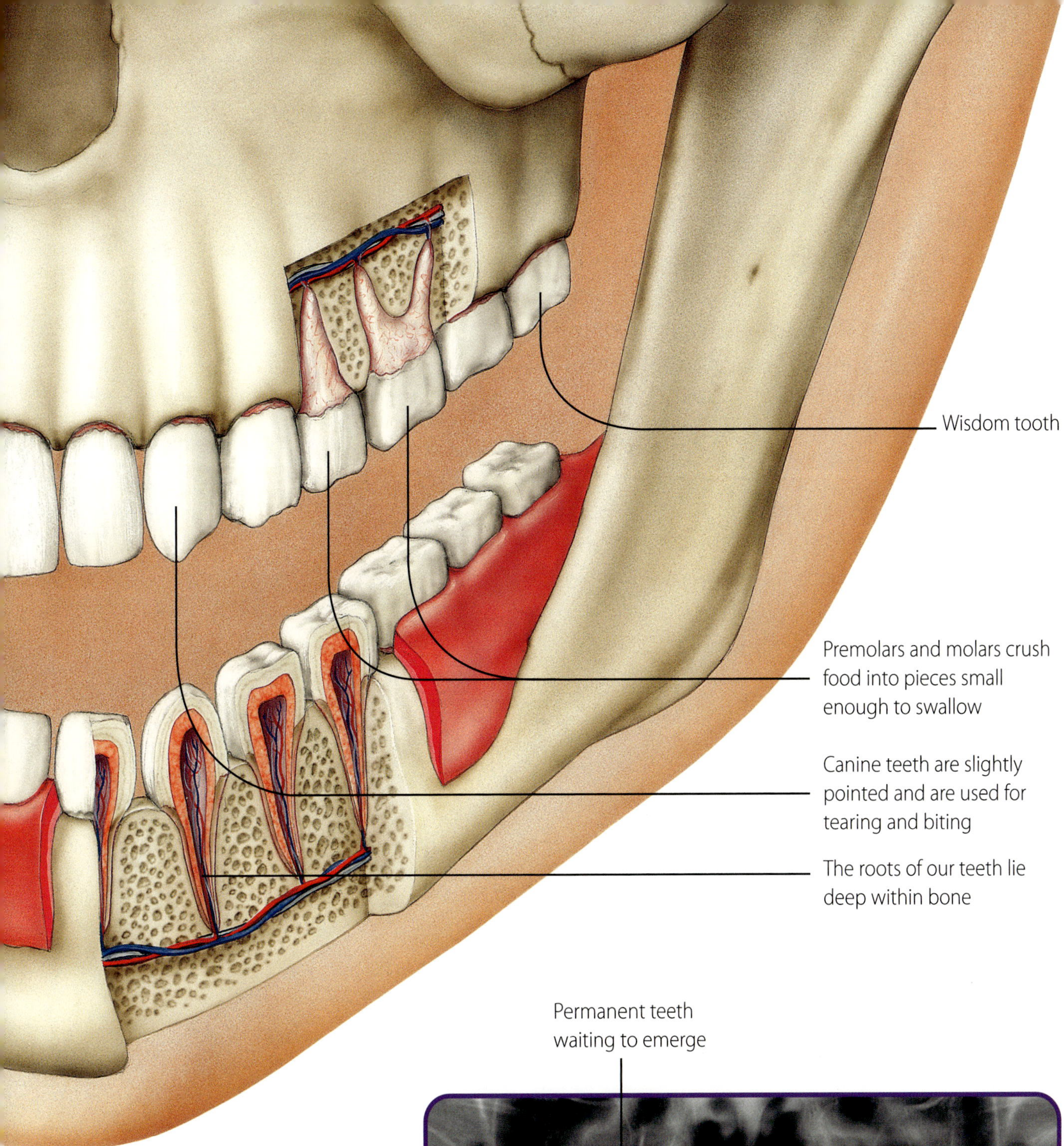

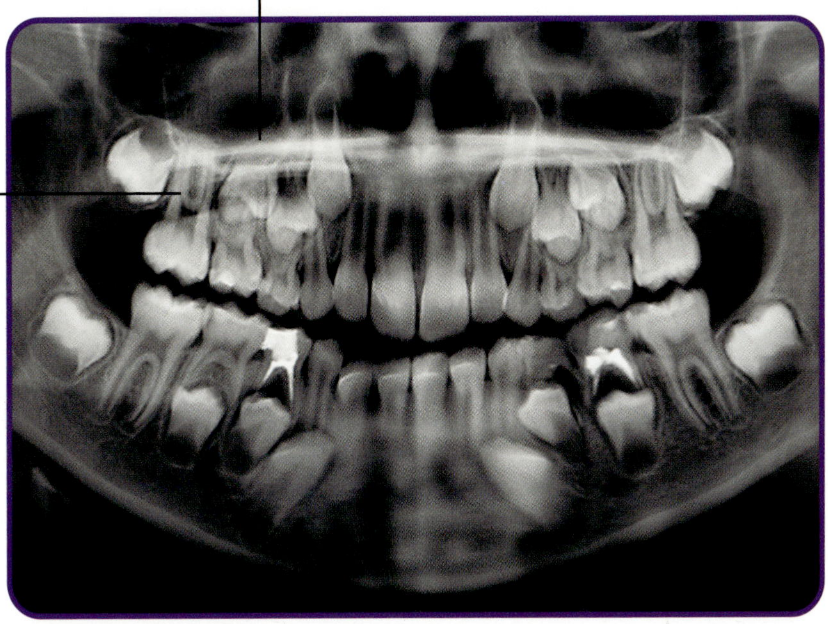

Dental X-rays

Dentists will sometimes X-ray our teeth. They do this for many reasons, such as: to find cavities that may need filling; to see abnormalities in the bone structure surrounding our teeth; or to check how teeth are developing, like in this picture (*see right*).

The Liver and Kidneys

The liver is the blood's cleaning and sorting center. A vein called the portal vein connects the intestines directly to the liver, bringing blood that is rich in dissolved food. The liver sorts through the materials in the blood, breaking down harmful chemicals, or toxins, as well as storing useful substances, such as sugars and vitamins.

When the kidneys receive blood containing dissolved waste substances, they filter and remove these along with any excess water. The kidneys pass this waste, or urine, to the bladder, and the clean, filtered blood flows back to the heart.

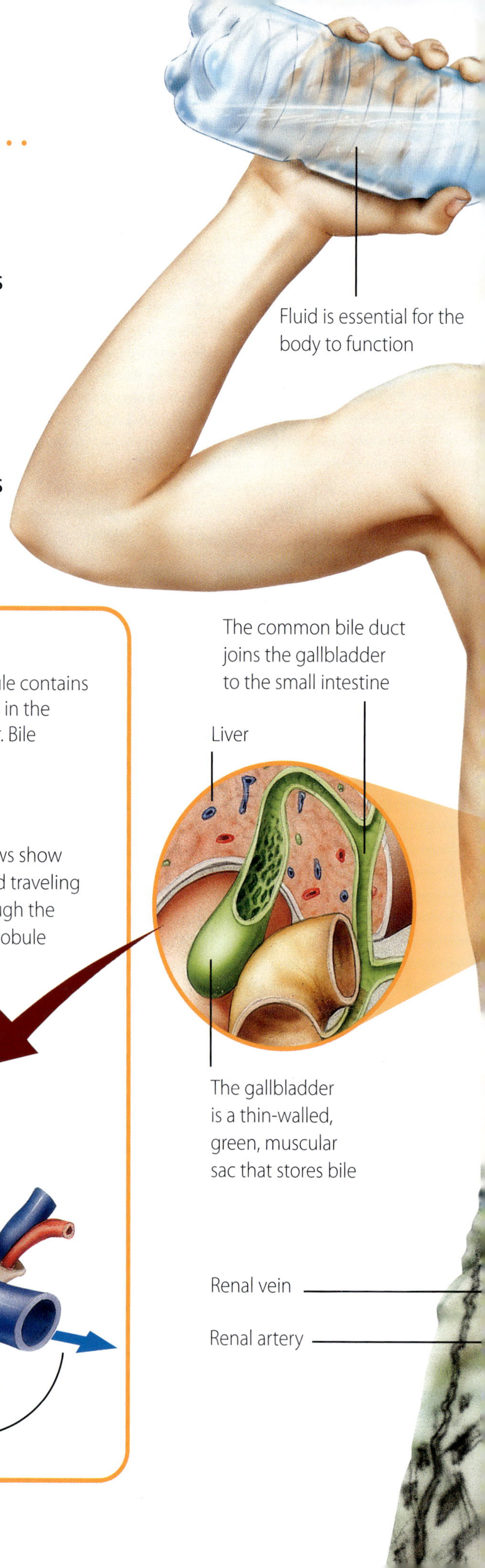

Liver lobules

Our liver is made up of small structures called lobules. Each lobule contains spaces through which blood flows. Some of the chemical waste in the blood is removed, turned into bile, and stored in the gallbladder. Bile removes waste and makes fats soluble for absorption.

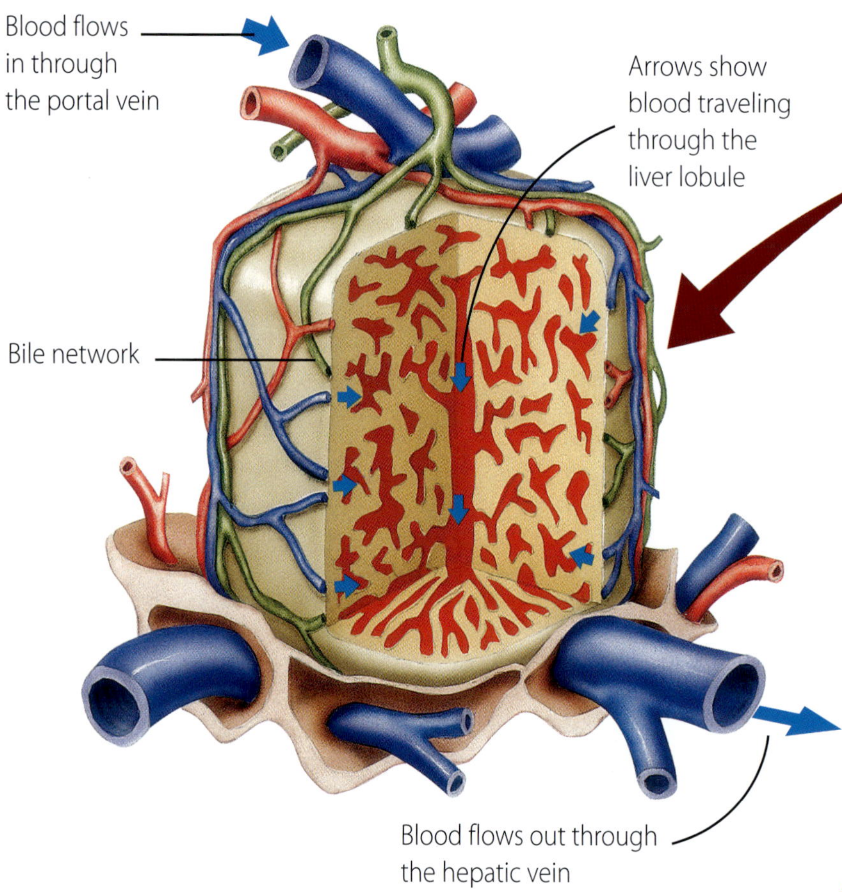

Nephrons

Our kidneys contain countless blood vessels surrounded by millions of tiny tubes called nephrons. These nephrons purify blood by removing waste substances. They also control the amount of water and salt in the blood. The waste, or urine, collects in the region of the kidneys called the renal pelvis, and travels down the ureters to the bladder.

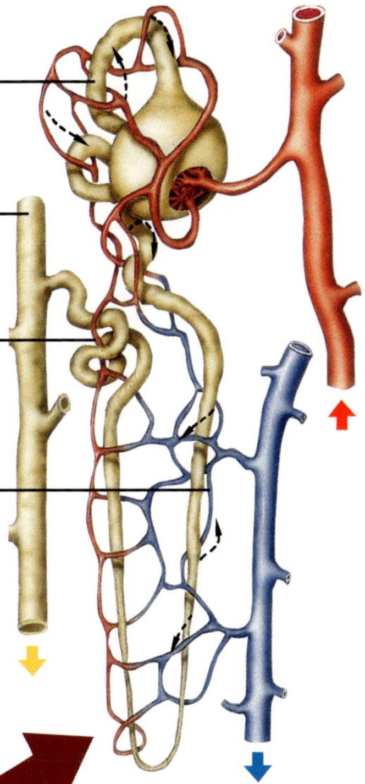

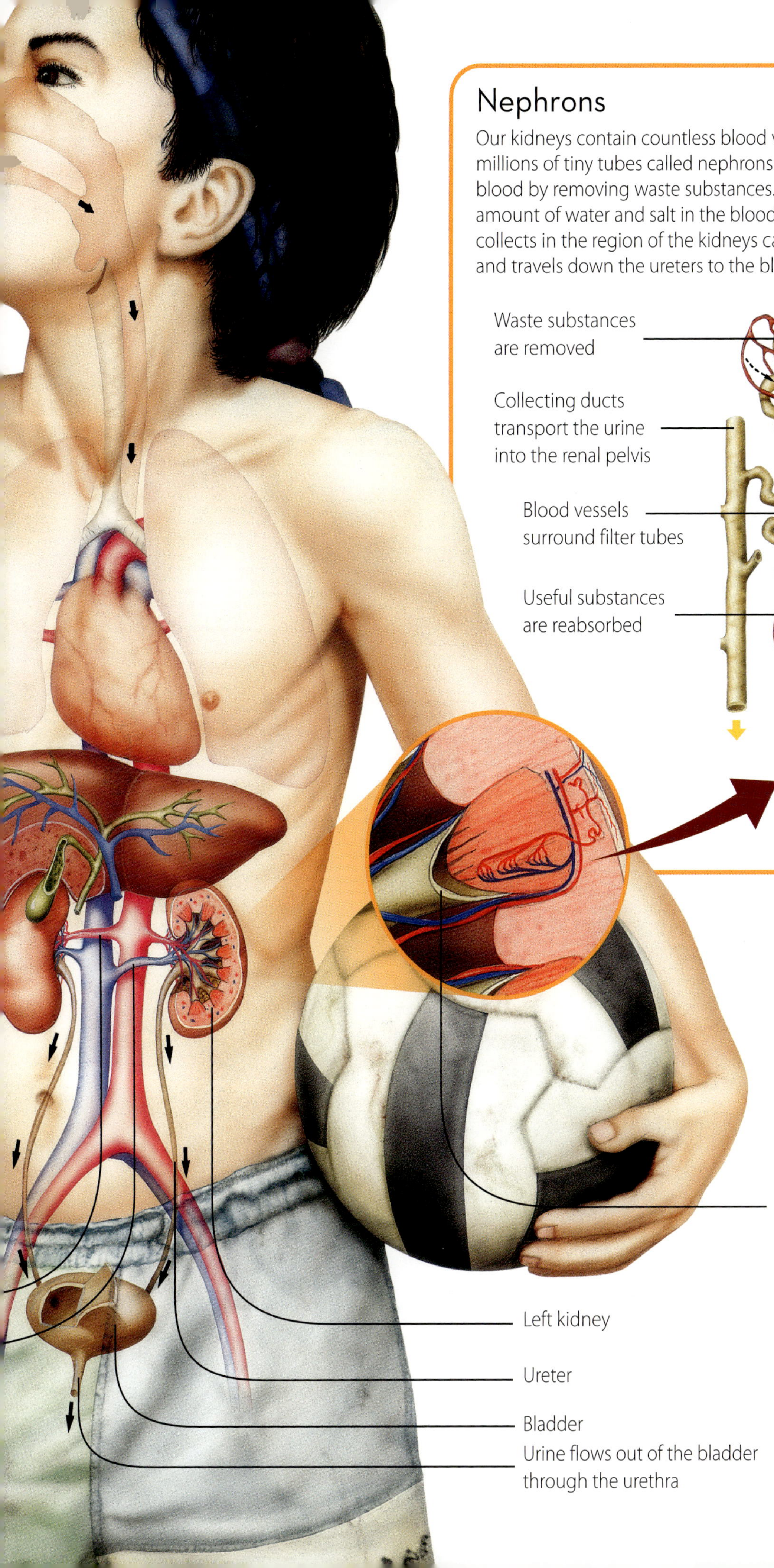

The Skin

Our skin is our protective "coat" – a complex covering made up of two layers. The top layer is the epidermis, which is waterproof and also protects us against germs. The cells in this layer are being shed all the time, with new cells growing in their place. The dermis layer beneath is much thicker, and is made up of stretchy, or elastic, fibers. It contains blood vessels, sweat glands, and hair roots, called follicles. These all help to control our body temperature. In hot weather, the blood vessels widen and allow more blood to flow near the surface of the skin. Sweat glands produce salty droplets that evaporate on the body and cool it down. In cold weather, muscles attached to hair follicles tighten, making our hairs stand on end. This traps a thin layer of warm air around the body. In addition, blood vessels narrow to keep the body's heat in and away from the skin's surface.

Nerve fibers in the skin

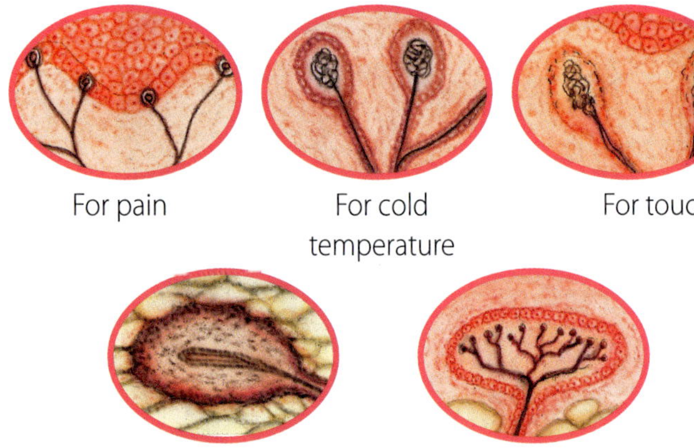

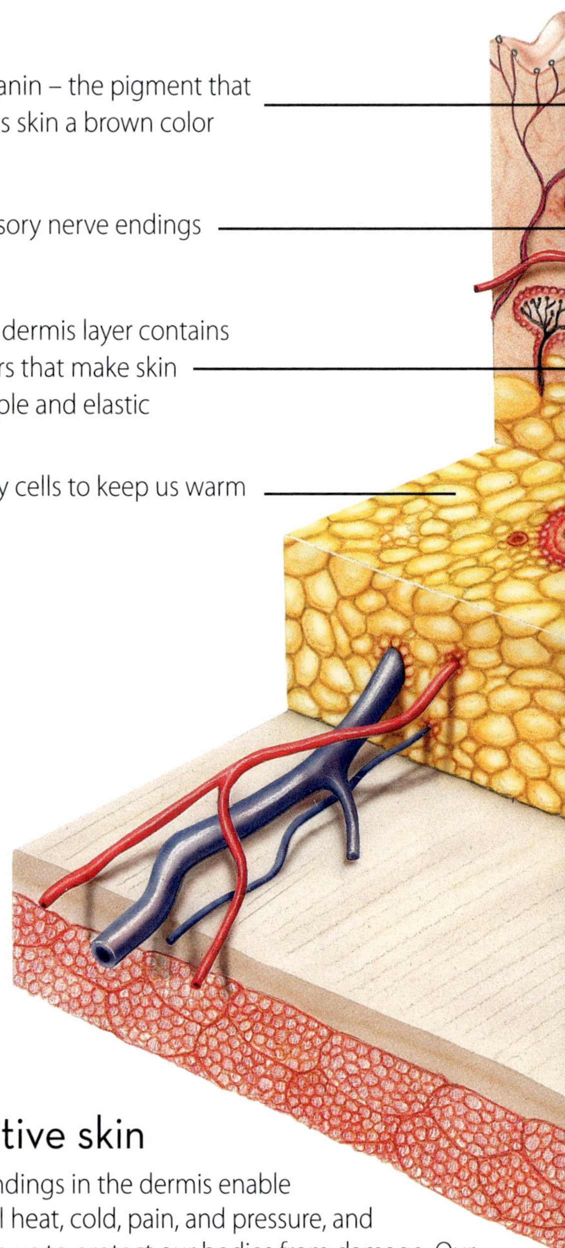

The sun

Our skin is delicate and sensitive to the ultraviolet rays in sunlight. If our skin is not protected, these rays can cause the skin to burn and may result in painful redness and blistering. Too much exposure can sometimes cause cells in our skin to change and skin cancer to develop.

Everybody needs to protect their skin from burning in the sun, either by staying in the shade, covering up, or using sunscreen. Sunscreen contains substances that help block out the harmful rays. Wearing a hat helps to protect our face and neck, and keeping our skin covered by clothing keeps the sun from damaging it.

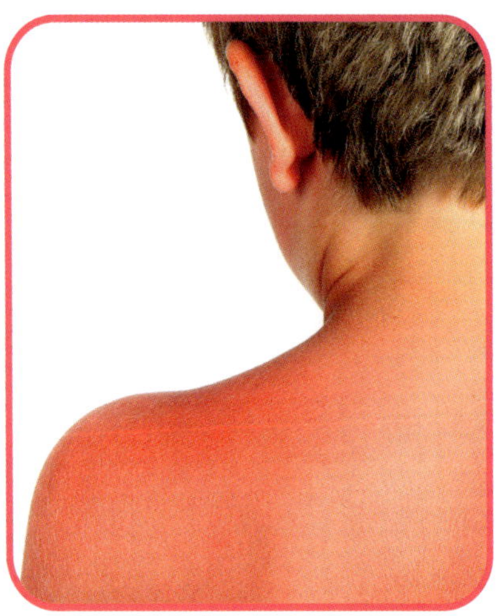

Sensitive skin

Nerve endings in the dermis enable us to feel heat, cold, pain, and pressure, and thus help us to protect our bodies from damage. Our hands, lips, and the soles of our feet are the most sensitive parts of our body because the skin on them has more nerve endings than other parts.

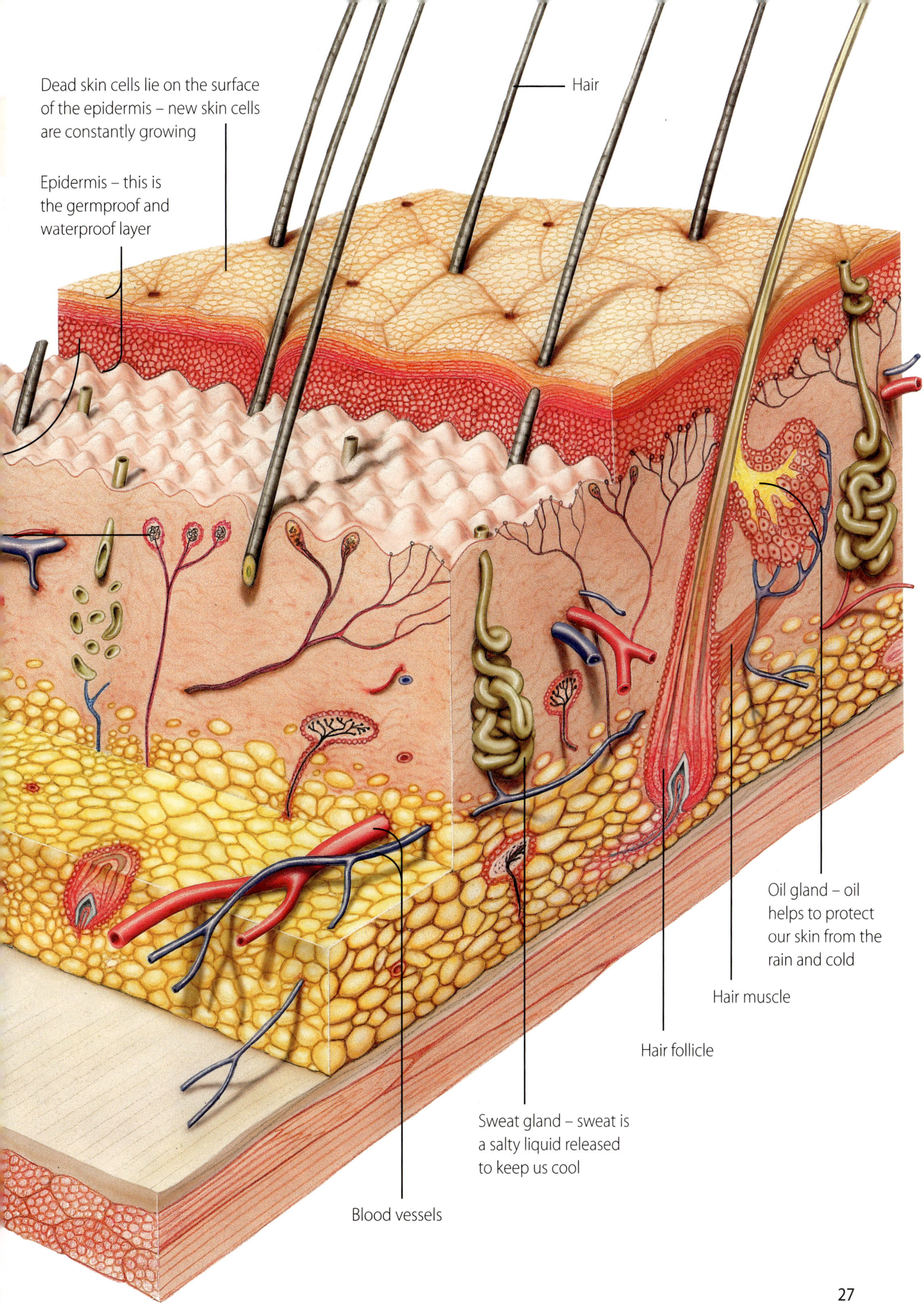
Dead skin cells lie on the surface of the epidermis – new skin cells are constantly growing
Hair
Epidermis – this is the germproof and waterproof layer
Oil gland – oil helps to protect our skin from the rain and cold
Hair muscle
Hair follicle
Sweat gland – sweat is a salty liquid released to keep us cool
Blood vessels

The Nerves

Our nervous system is a busy network of nerves. It includes the nerves in our brain and the nerves that stretch throughout our bodies. Our brain is connected to the rest of our body by the spinal cord, a bundle of nerves and cells that runs down through the spinal column.

Nerves are made up of thin strands called neurons. There are millions of these throughout the nervous system and each consists of a cell body, which has short branches called dendrites. The long arm of the neuron is called the axon. Some axons are enclosed in a fatty layer called myelin, which helps to speed up the conduction, or passing, of nerve messages along the axon. Nerve cells in our spinal cord cannot be replaced so spinal injury can be serious, although research into stem cell replacement therapy may find new ways to help repair it.

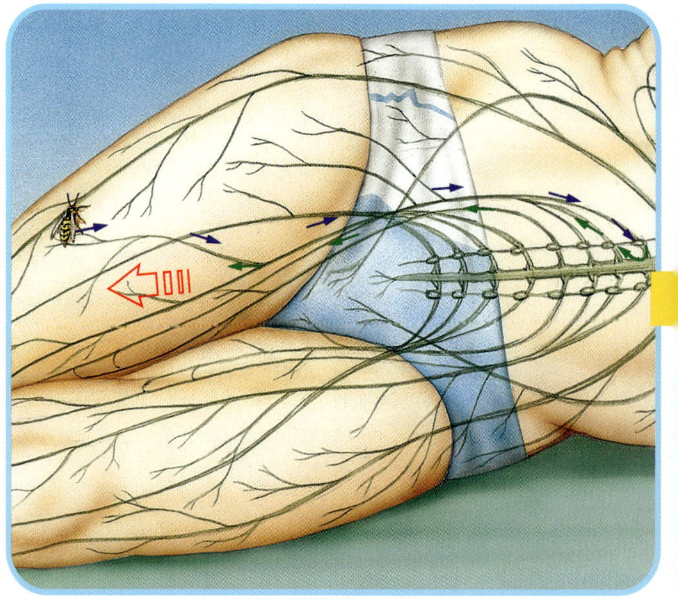

The reflex action

The sensory impulse travels from the site of the pain and into the spinal cord. It is then transmitted to neurons in the gray matter of the cord, which link up with motor neurons. The impulse travels back down the leg in the motor nerve and the leg muscle tightens, making the leg jerk. This is called a "reflex action" and does not involve the brain.

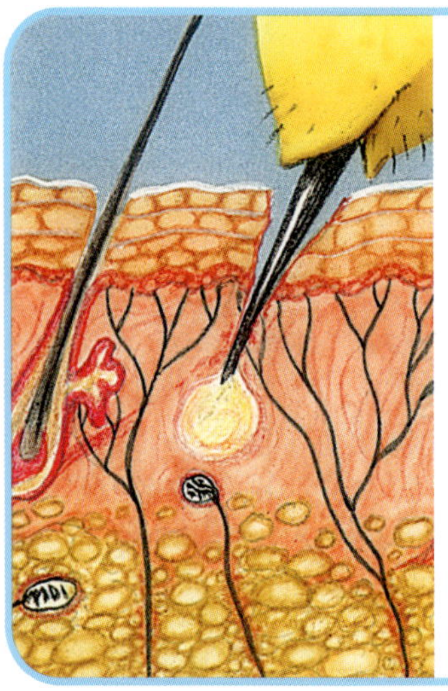

A wasp sting

When a wasp stings, nerve endings in the area send a nerve message, called an impulse, along the nerve cell and on to the spinal cord. Nerves carrying sensations, such as pain, are known as sensory nerves.

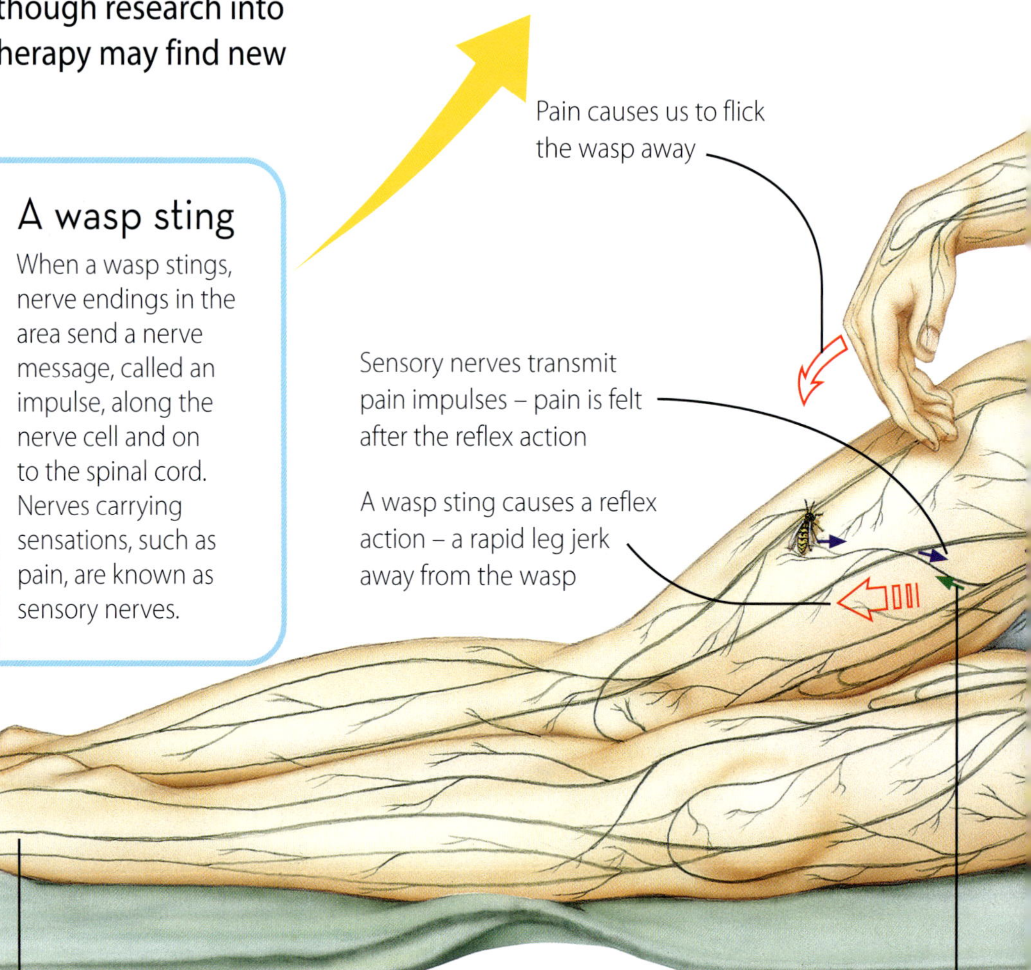

Communication network

This picture shows a series of neurons. Nerve impulses pass between neurons by jumping across a gap called a synapse. When an impulse reaches the end of an axon, chemicals are released that allow it to pass across the synapse and on to the next neuron.

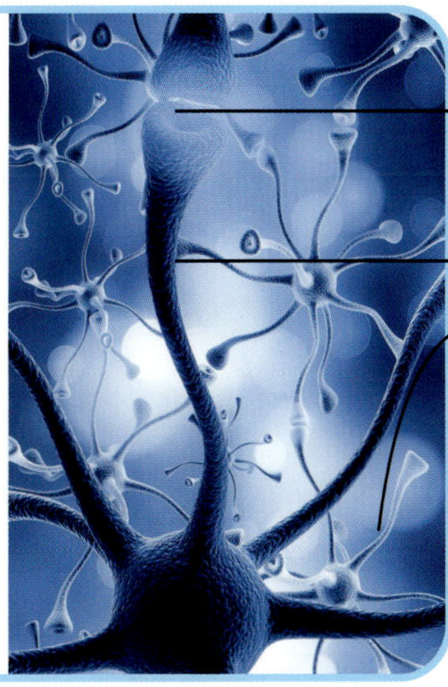

The motor end plate

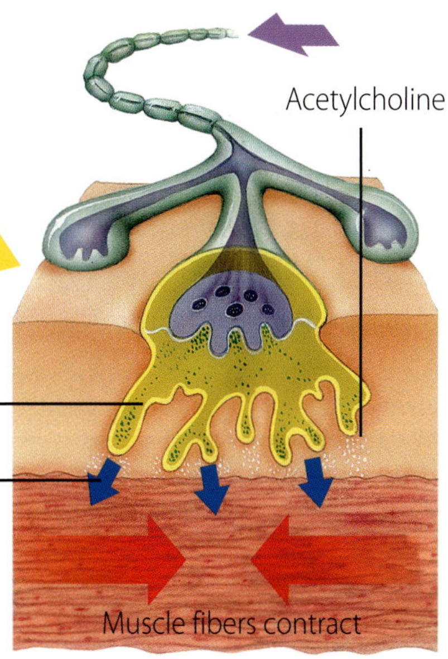

The axon of a motor neuron meets the muscle at a special junction called the motor end plate. When the nerve impulse is received at the motor end plate, a substance called acetylcholine is released. This sticks to the outside of the muscle fiber, causing "gates" in the muscle fiber to open and let in sodium. This activity makes the muscle contract and movement occurs.

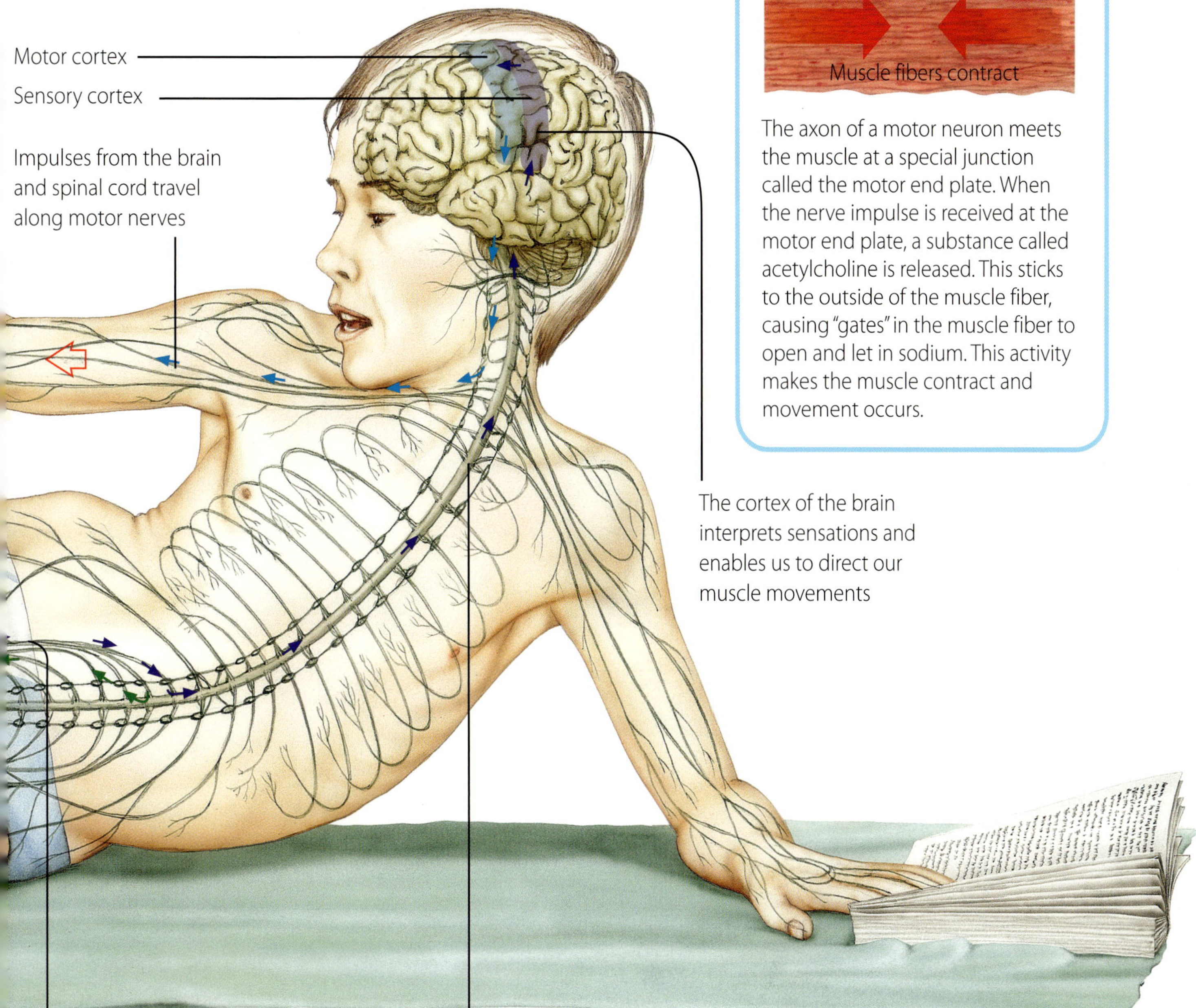

The Brain

The brain looks like a mass of wrinkled, grayish jelly and is very soft. It is protected in the hard, bony case called the skull. The human brain is relatively large. The wrinkles make it compact, in spite of its large surface area.

The brain is the body's control center. It is involved with what we do and what we think, as well as what we feel and remember. We also use our brain to learn. The left-hand side of our brain controls the right side of the body, and the right-hand side of our brain controls the left side of the body. Most people are right-handed because the left side of the brain is generally used more than the right side. Each side of our brain is responsible for different skills – the right side holds our artistic talent and imagination, while the left side is more responsible for practical abilities and logical thinking.

Right Side

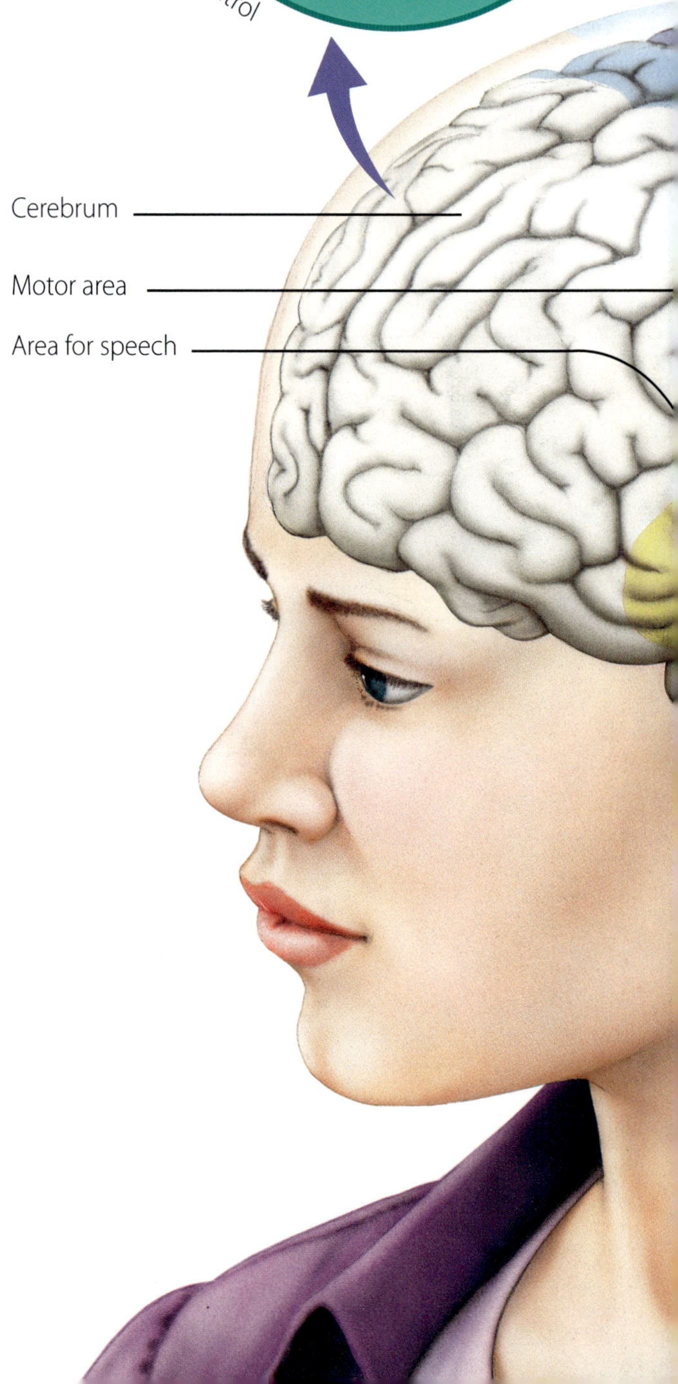

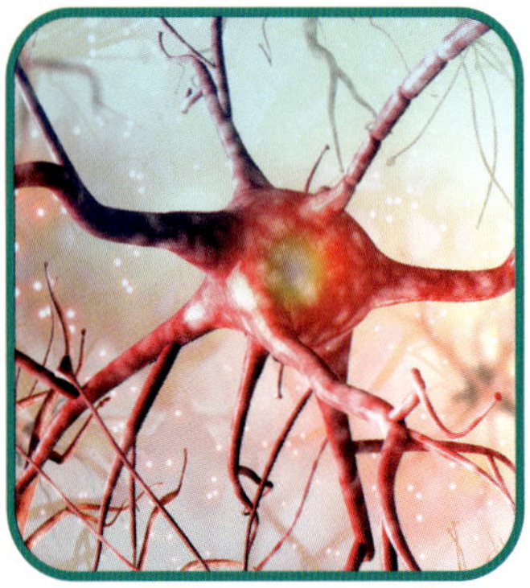

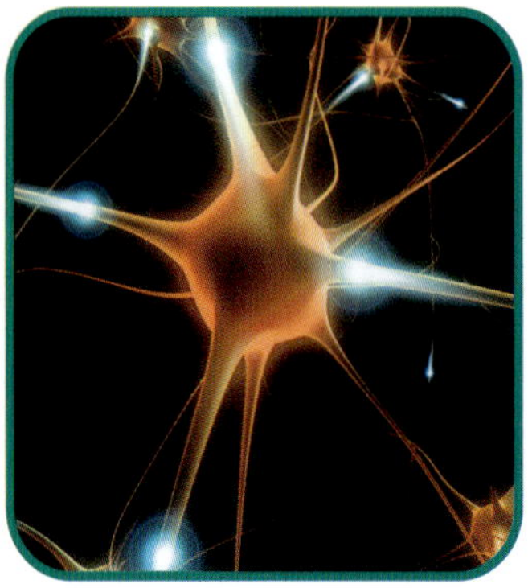

Brain cells

The cells that make up the brain are called neurons *(above left)*. Branches from the cells, called dendrites, receive impulses from the nerves, while axons transmit them *(above right)*. Our brain interprets the impulses and can tell where they are coming from and what they mean. The brain cells can also store information. A piece of stored information is called a memory. One part of our brain stores long-term memories, another part more recent, or short-term, memories.

Left Side

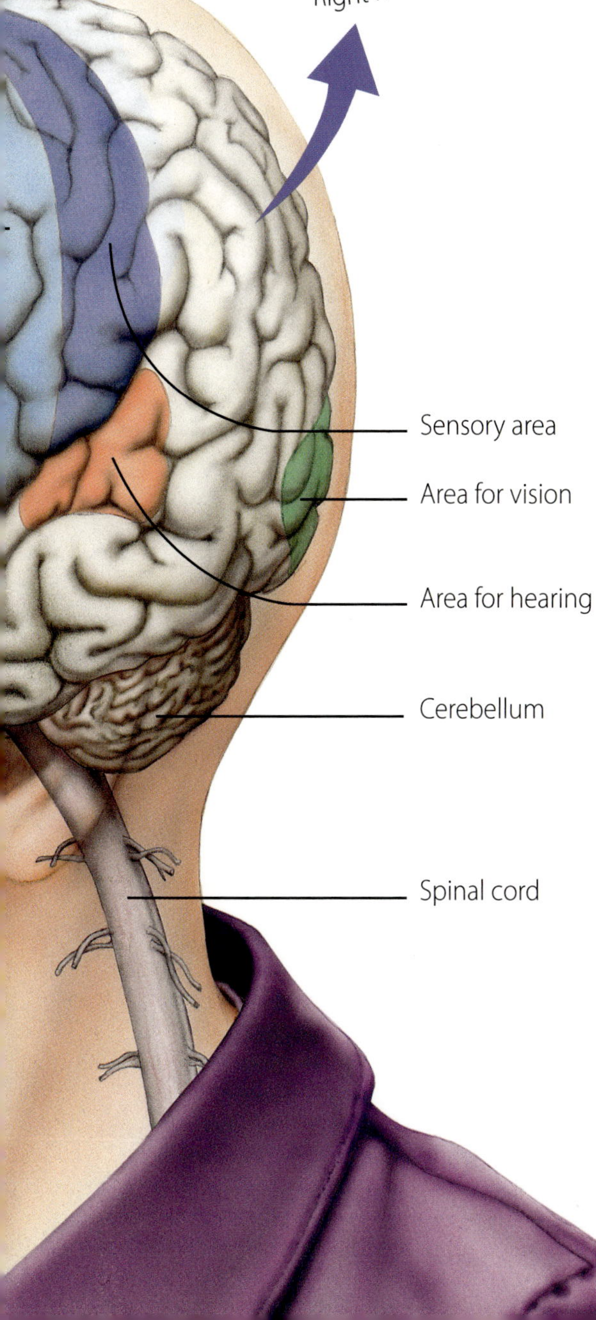

The cerebrum

The largest part of the brain consists of two sections. Together they are known as the cerebral hemispheres, or cerebrum *(below)*. The cerebrum is highly organized. It is arranged in areas that relate to different parts of the body and to different needs. Vision is interpreted at the back of the cerebrum, hearing and speech at the side. The areas for sensation and movement are in the middle. The area at the front of the cerebrum, the frontal lobe, controls our behavior. Below and to the back of the cerebrum lies the cerebellum. It contains nerve cells that are mainly concerned with balance. Below this, the brain is connected to the rest of the body by the spinal cord.

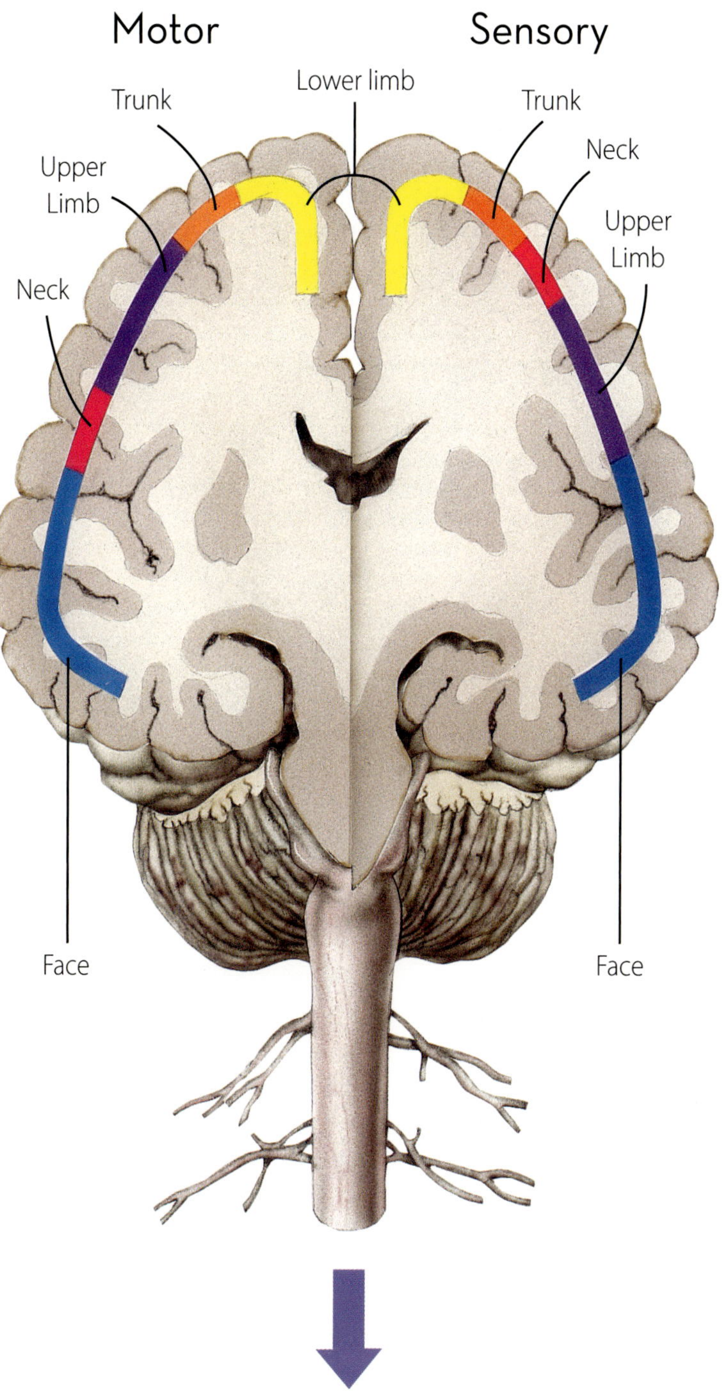

Seeing

Our eyes work like cameras. Each eye has a pupil, which, similar to a camera's aperture, is a hole that allows light to enter the eye. When it is dark, our pupils enlarge to let in as much light as possible. The size of each pupil is controlled by the iris, which surrounds it. When light passes through the pupil, it meets the lens. The lens causes the light to bend so that it shines on an area at the back of the eye called the retina. The retina is something like the color film or sensor chip in a camera, in that an image can be formed on it. This image is upside down and is transmitted by the optic nerve to the brain, which enables us to interpret it the right way up.

Focusing with glasses

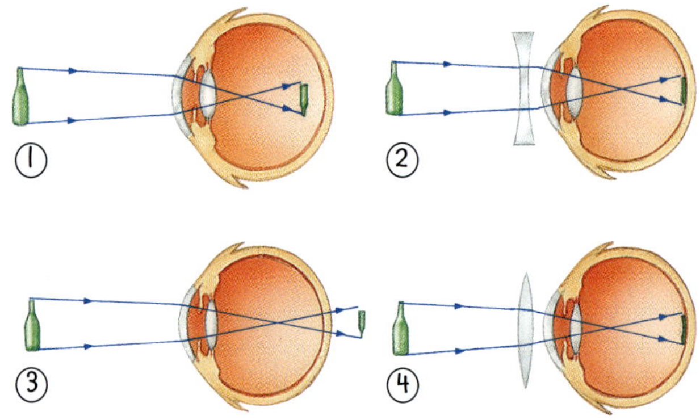

A traditional camera can be focused by moving the lens in and out, but the human eye focuses by making its lens thinner and longer or shorter and thicker. Some people's lenses do not focus properly, but their vision can be improved by wearing glasses or contact lenses. These provide another lens through which the light is bent, allowing it to focus accurately on the retina. Nearsighted people cannot see distant objects clearly because their eyes focus them in front of the retina (**1**). Concave lenses are used to correct this (**2**). Farsighted people cannot see close objects clearly because their eyes focus them behind the retina (**3**). These people need convex lenses (**4**).

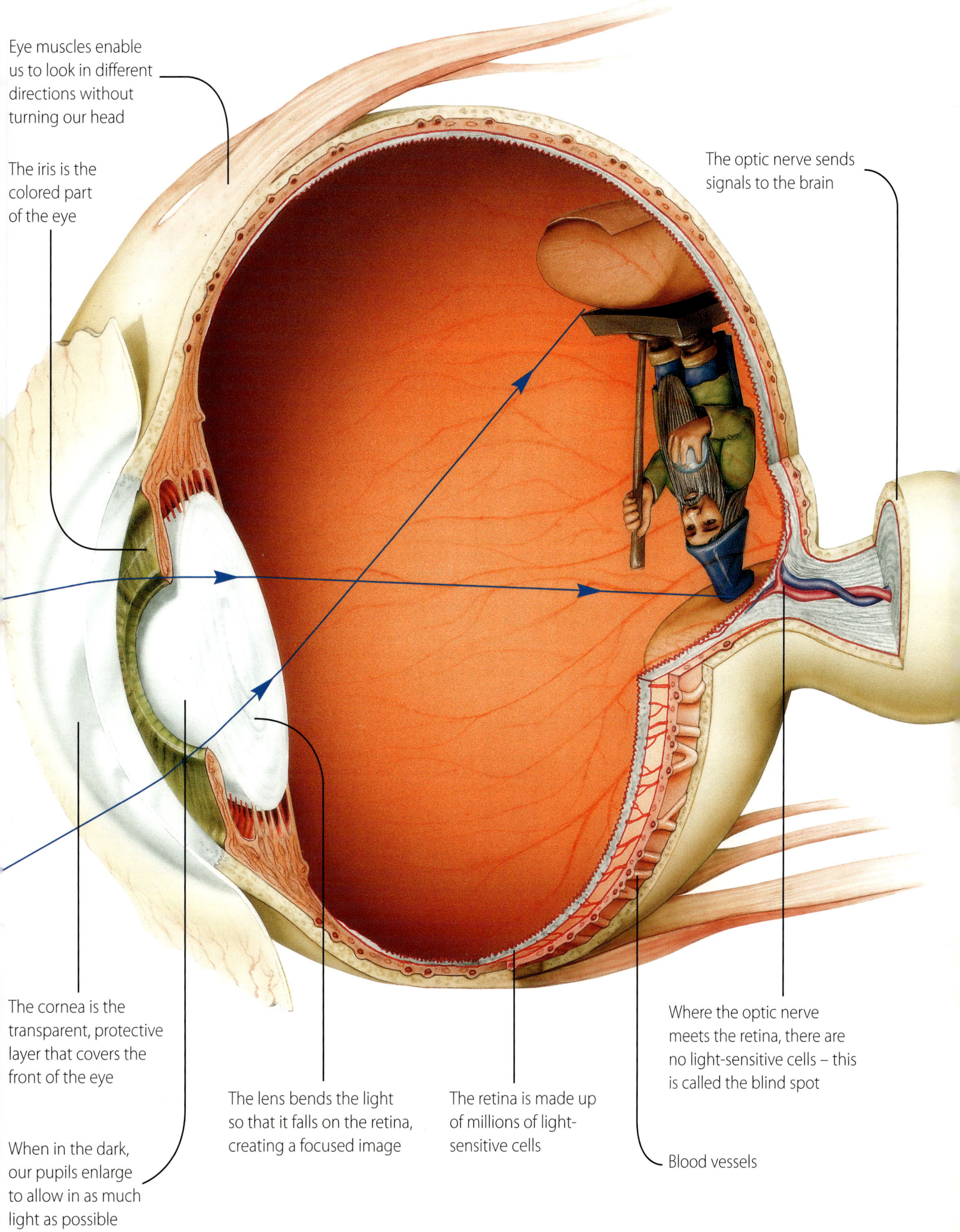
Eye muscles enable us to look in different directions without turning our head
The iris is the colored part of the eye
The optic nerve sends signals to the brain
The cornea is the transparent, protective layer that covers the front of the eye
When in the dark, our pupils enlarge to allow in as much light as possible
The lens bends the light so that it falls on the retina, creating a focused image
The retina is made up of millions of light-sensitive cells
Where the optic nerve meets the retina, there are no light-sensitive cells – this is called the blind spot
Blood vessels

Taste and Smell

We are most familiar with the senses of taste and smell for the pleasure they can bring. However, they probably developed to protect us from eating food that could be poisonous. Our sense of smell is much stronger than our sense of taste. When we taste food, we rely on the smell and texture as well as the flavor. This is why we cannot taste food very well when we have a blocked or runny nose.

When eating a pear, for example, scent from the fruit rises up the nose and dissolves in a mucus lining that covers the scent-sensitive cells at the top of the nose. Nerve signals are sent from the cells to the olfactory lobe in the brain, where the smell is recognized and enjoyed. The pear's sweetness is also sensed by taste buds on the tongue, and is similarly transmitted by nerve signals to the brain.

Odor-sensitive cells

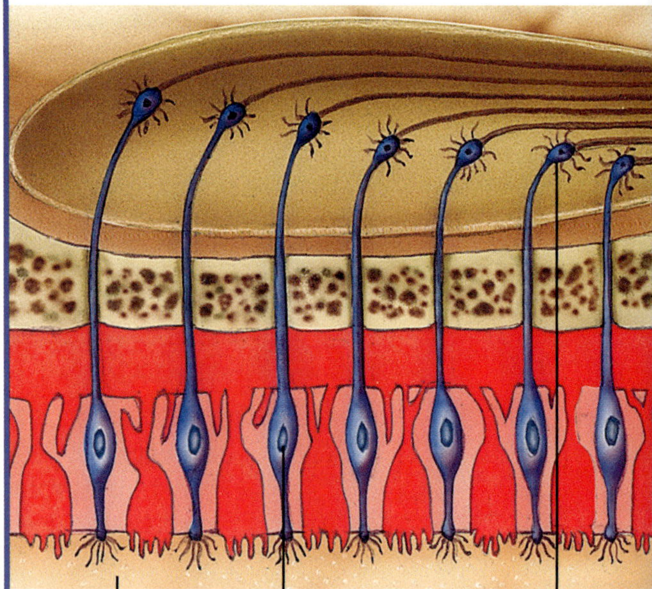

At the top of our nose lie special odor-sensitive cells that become stimulated when scents are released from food, drinks, and our surroundings. These special cells are called olfactory cells and they contain hairs that are covered with mucus. Scents dissolve in the mucus, causing nerve impulses to be sent to the brain.

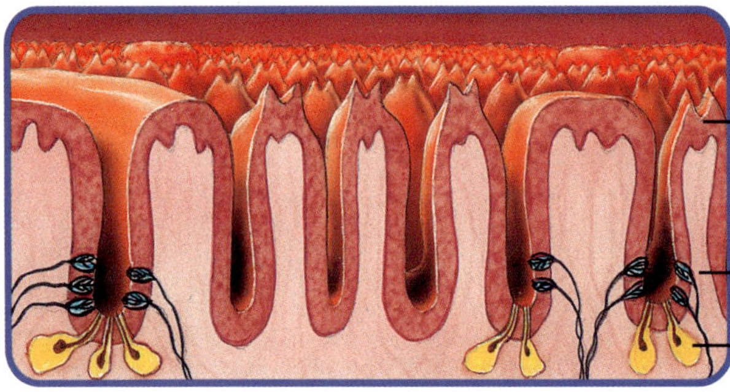

Five kinds of taste

Our tongue and the inside of our mouth are covered by about 10,000 taste buds. They detect salt, sweet, sour, savory, or bitter flavors in food that dissolve in the fluid – or saliva – in our mouth. The information that the taste buds provide to the brain enables us to distinguish a wide range of subtle flavors.

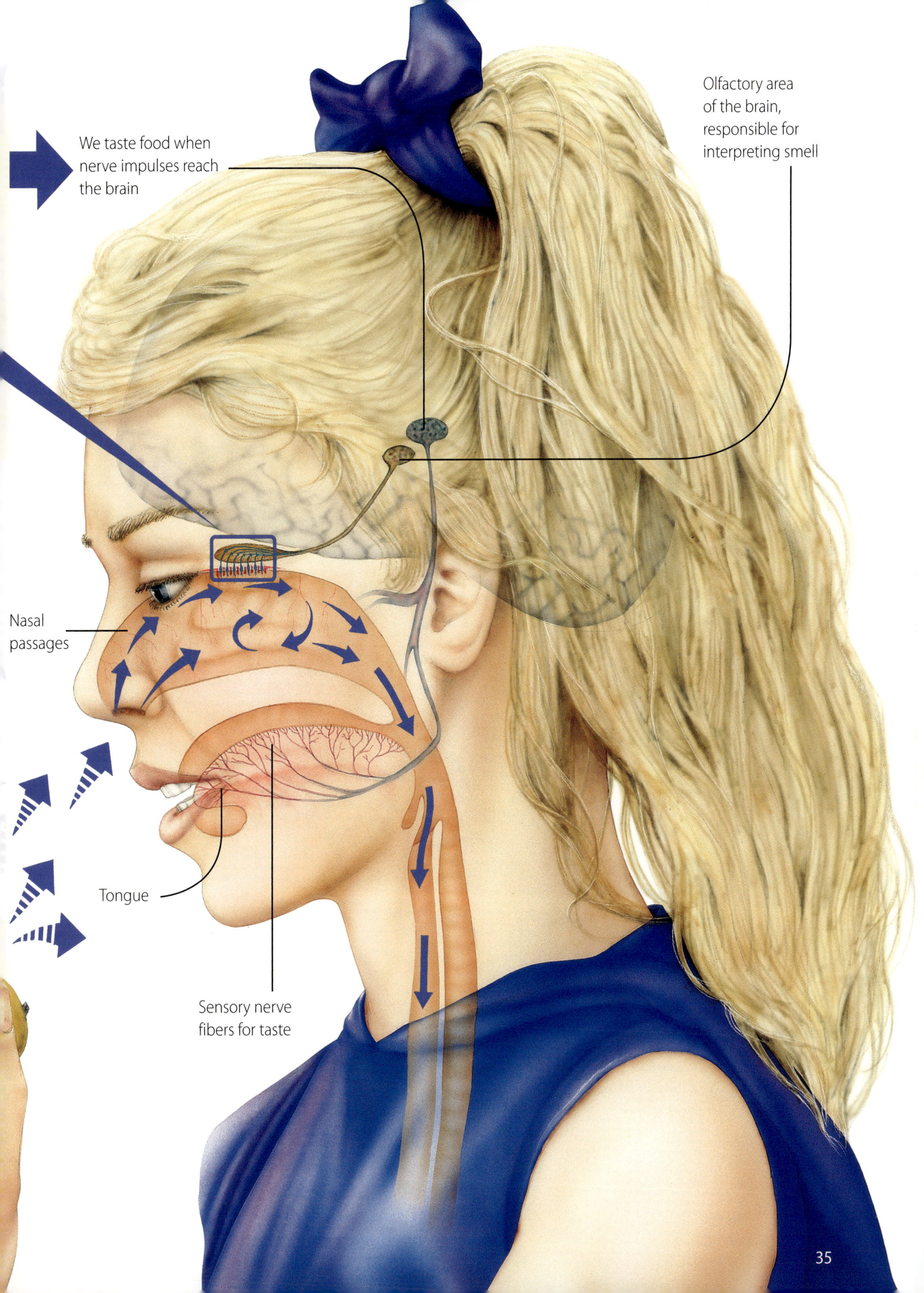
Olfactory area
of the brain,
responsible for
interpreting smell
We taste food when
nerve impulses reach
the brain
Nasal
passages
Tongue
Sensory nerve
fibers for taste

Hearing

The part of the ear we can see is shaped to collect sound and allow it to travel along the ear canal to the eardrum. Sound waves cause the eardrum to vibrate. Behind the eardrum are three small bones called the hammer, anvil, and stirrup, which get their names from their shapes. Vibrations from the eardrum cause these small bones to vibrate too, and these vibrations pass through an oval window to the cochlea.

The cochlea is a coiled tube filled with liquid. Low-pitched sounds make the first part of the tube vibrate, while high-pitched sounds vibrate a part further along. These vibrations are picked up by nerve fibers connected to the brain. The brain can tell where the vibrations are occurring, and can tell one sound from another.

Balance and sound

Our ears also help us to balance. There are three semicircular canals in the ear. They contain fluid that moves when we change our position. The moving fluid sends signals to the brain that help our body adjust and keep its sense of balance.

Our ears can tolerate very loud sounds, but if they are too loud, the cochlea can become damaged. Soft sounds become more difficult to hear as we get older. We can hear low- and high-pitched sounds, although many animals, such as bats, can hear much higher-pitched sounds than we can.

Cross-section of cochlea tubes

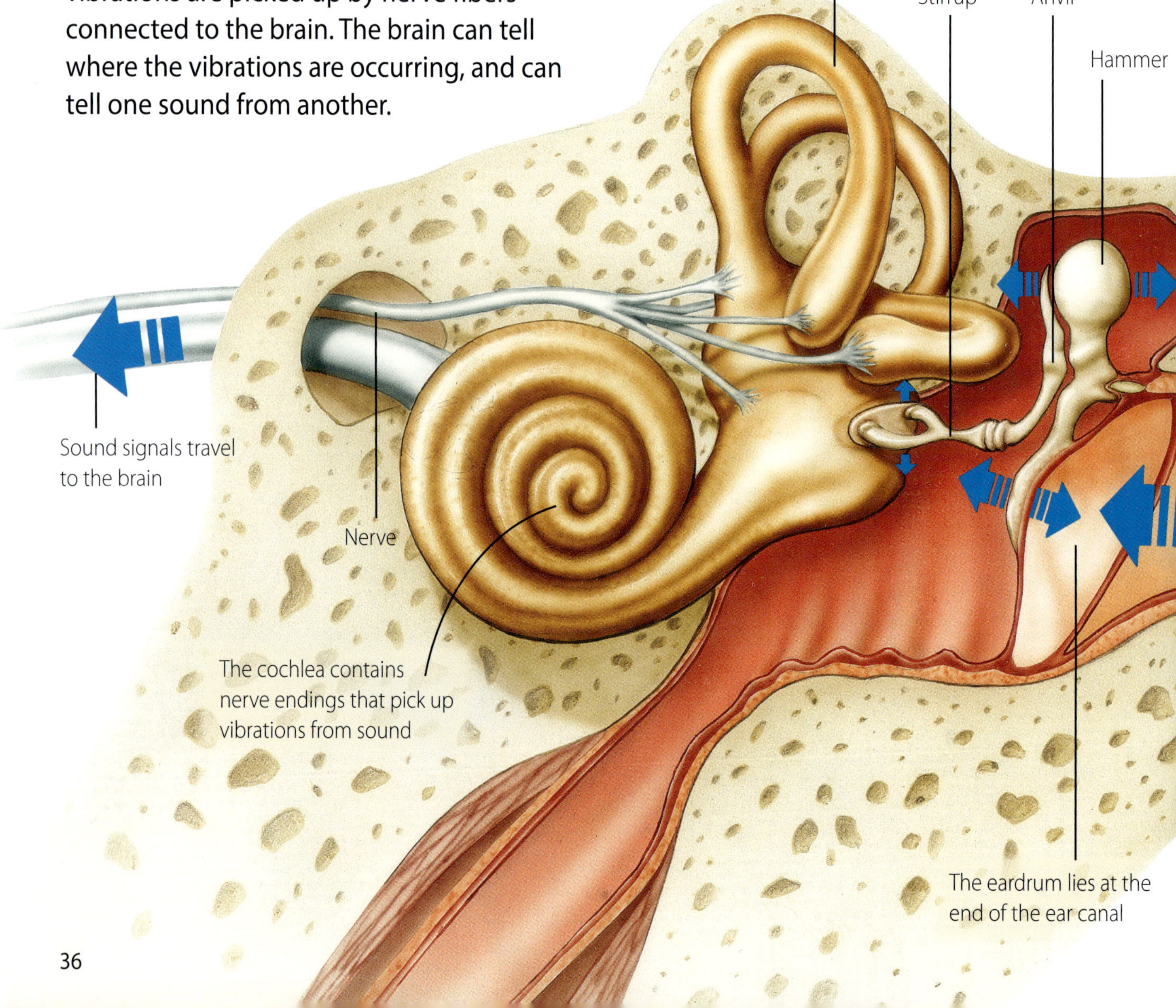

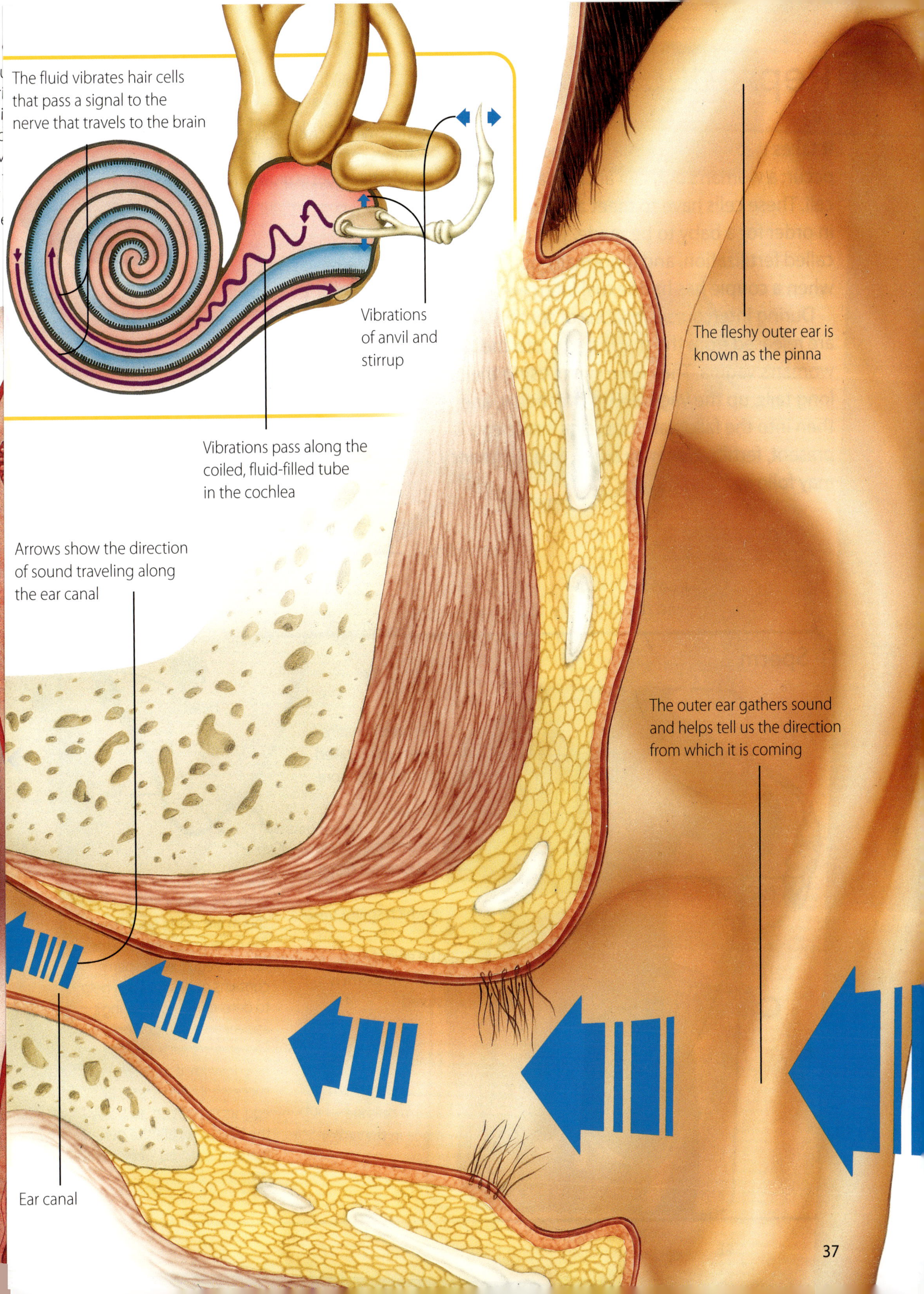
The fluid vibrates hair cells that pass a signal to the nerve that travels to the brain
Vibrations of anvil and stirrup
The fleshy outer ear is known as the pinna
Vibrations pass along the coiled, fluid-filled tube in the cochlea
Arrows show the direction of sound traveling along the ear canal
The outer ear gathers sound and helps tell us the direction from which it is coming
Ear canal

Fighting Germs

Millions of bacteria and viruses live on and in our body. These germs don't usually harm us because they cannot easily pass through our skin or the acid in our stomach. However, if they do get past these barriers, white cells protect us. Most white cells are contained in lymph tissue, such as the tonsils and spleen, as well as in our blood. There are several different types of white cells that make up the immune system. The most common are the polymorphs, which destroy germs. Sometimes, germs have protective coatings to help them avoid being attacked by polymorphs. When this happens, our bodies produce specially shaped structures called antibodies that lock into the germ's coating, breaking them apart.

Destroying a germ

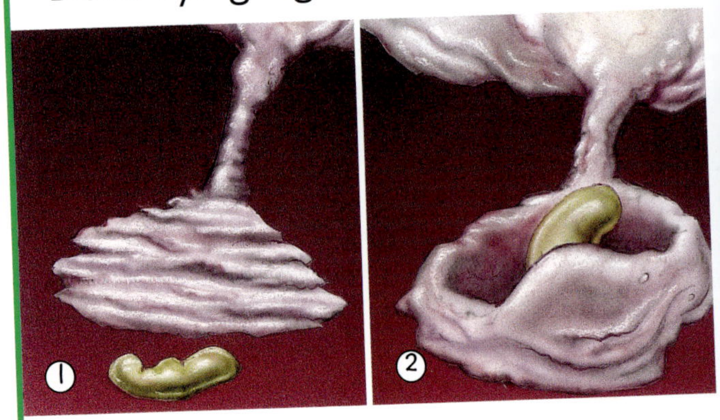

These pictures show how a polymorph white cell works. A chemical message alerts it to the presence of a harmful bacterium. The polymorph moves to where the bacterium is and makes part of its cell longer (**1**). This elongated part then surrounds the bacterium (**2**). Next, the polymorph cell membrane closes around the

Immunization

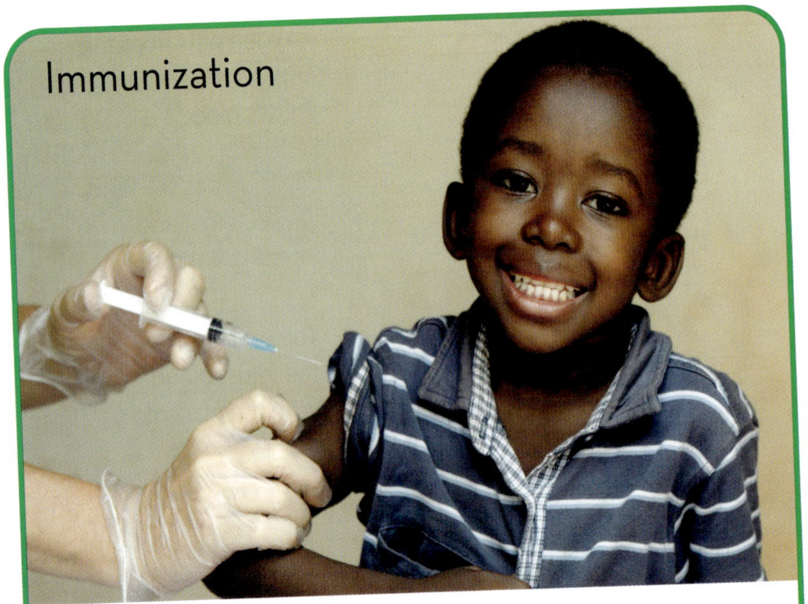

Many diseases that used to be very common are rare in developed countries today. This is because many people receive vaccines against these diseases, often when they are children, either by injection or by mouth.

Most vaccinations put dead or weakened germs into our bodies. These germs are not harmful enough to make us very ill, but they cause our immune system to produce antibodies that protect us from an attack by live, disease-causing germs. The biggest worldwide vaccination program ever began in 2020 to immunize against COVID-19 during a global pandemic.

Eggs and fertilization

Women usually release one egg each month from one of their two ovaries. The egg is released from the ovary into the fallopian tube, which is where fertilization occurs. Once a sperm penetrates the egg by breaking through its outer wall, other sperm are then prevented from entering the egg. The sperm and egg join together to form a cell that divides, again and again, to form a clump of cells that attaches to the wall of the uterus. This soon forms an embryo, which grows into a fetus.

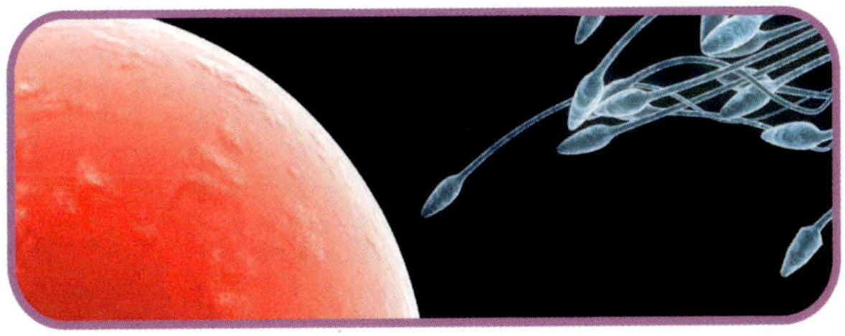

The sperm fertilizes the egg (*above*) in the fallopian tube

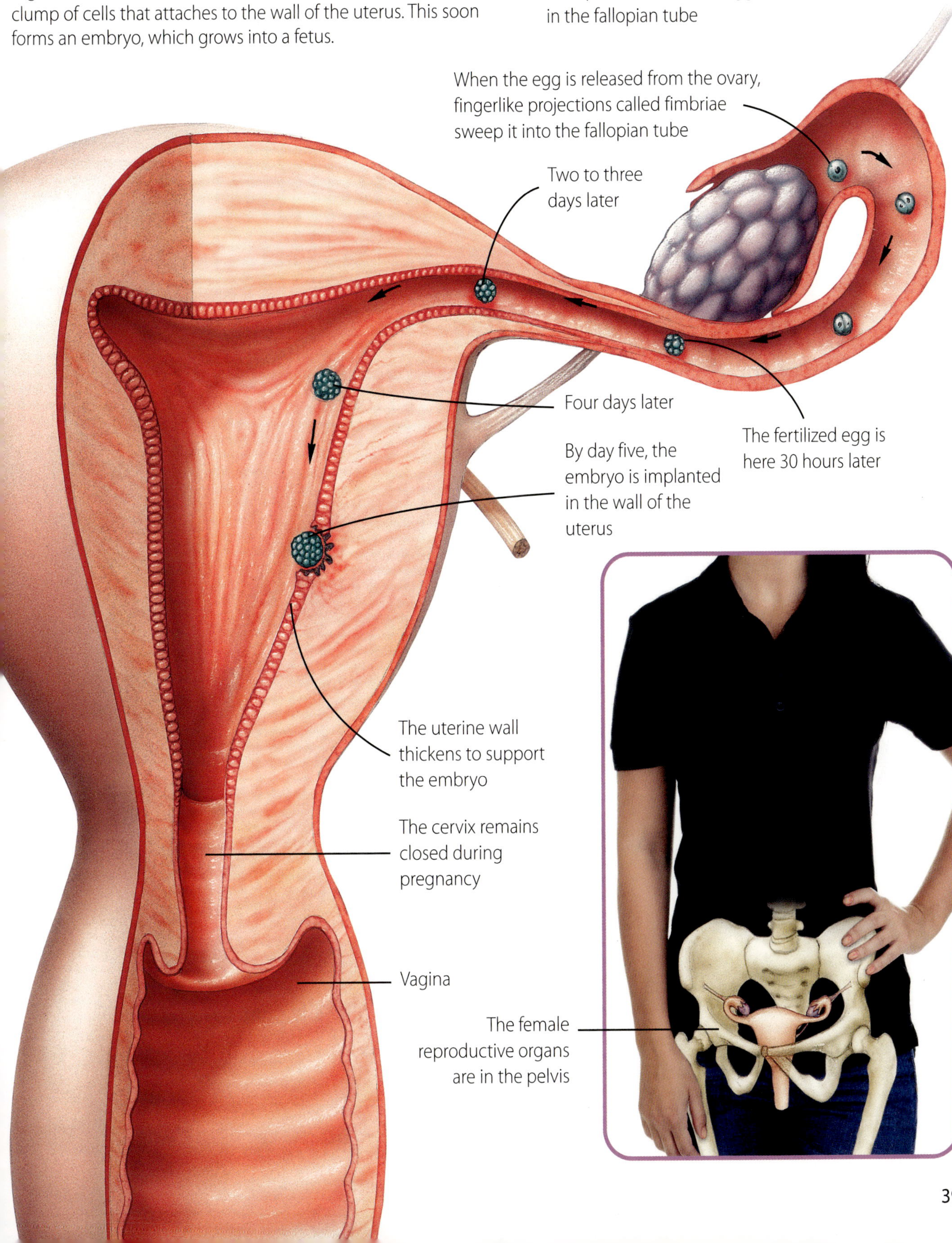

The female reproductive organs are in the pelvis

How a Baby Grows

Each of us begins life as a tiny, microscopic cell. Over the course of just nine months, this single cell becomes a baby, fully formed and ready to be born. First, inside the mother, the cell divides into a hollow ball of many cells. This becomes attached to the side of the mother's uterus, and grows into what we call the fetus. The head soon grows, the arms and legs form, and the fetus begins to look like a human being. A tube, called the umbilical cord, connects the fetus to the placenta on the wall of the uterus. When the baby is ready to be born, chemicals signal the mother's uterus to push the baby out. The umbilical cord is then cut, leaving the newborn baby with a small scar – the belly button.

Stages of growth

To survive and grow, the fetus needs nutrition and oxygen from its mother, and to be able to get rid of waste. This happens inside the placenta, where many blood vessels allow dissolved nutrients and oxygen from the mother's blood to transfer to the blood of the fetus, while waste chemicals from the fetus's blood are transported away by the mother's blood.

After two months, the main parts of the body are formed. At this stage, the fetus looks rather strange, as its head seems too big for its body. At five months, the toenails, fingernails, and all the main organs have formed, and the eyelashes have appeared.

By seven and a half months, the fetus looks like a small version of a newborn baby. It is about 15 inches (38 cm) long, while at birth a baby is usually about 20 inches (50 cm) long. Babies born at this earlier stage are usually able to survive if given special medical care. When a baby is born early it is called premature.

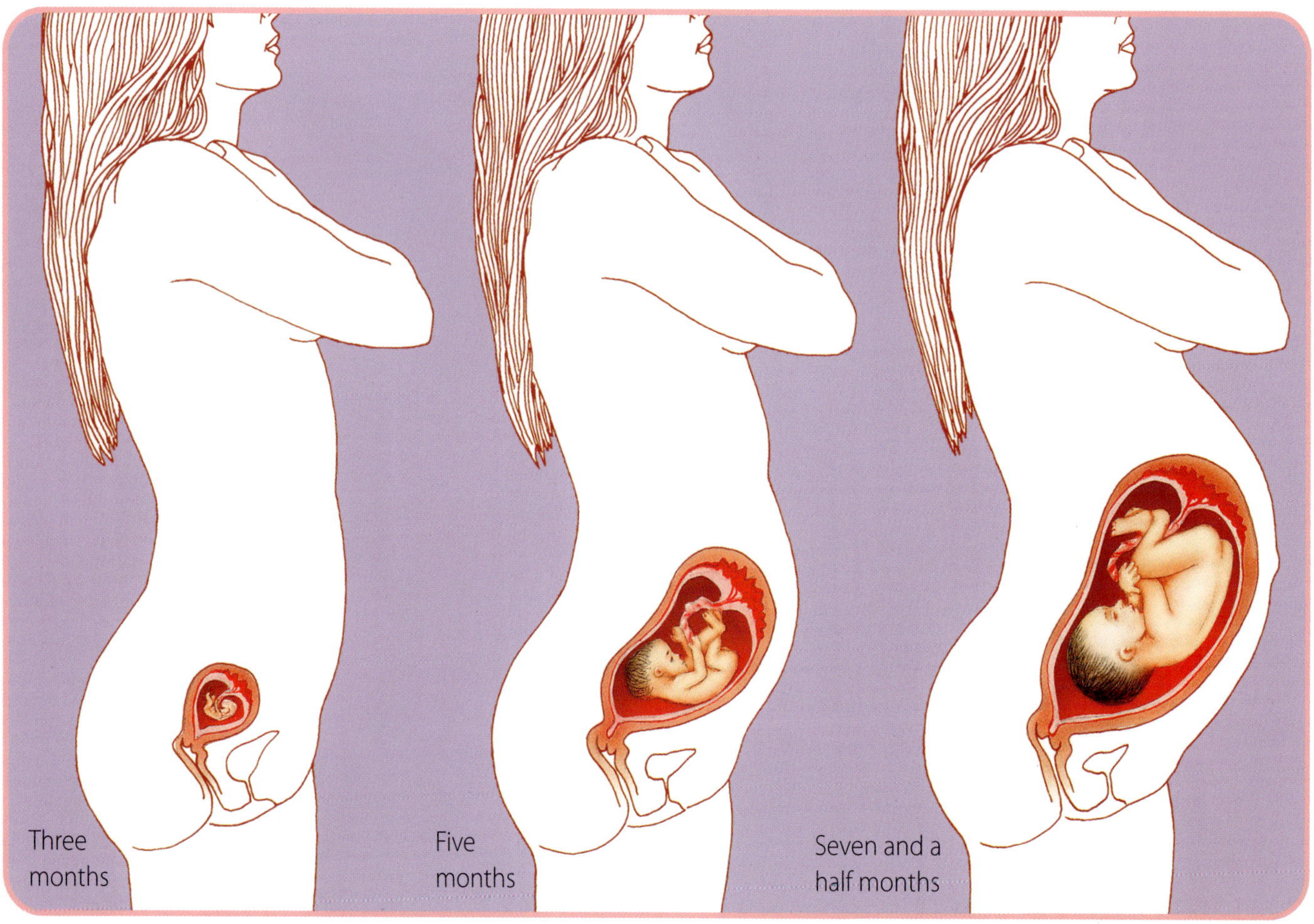

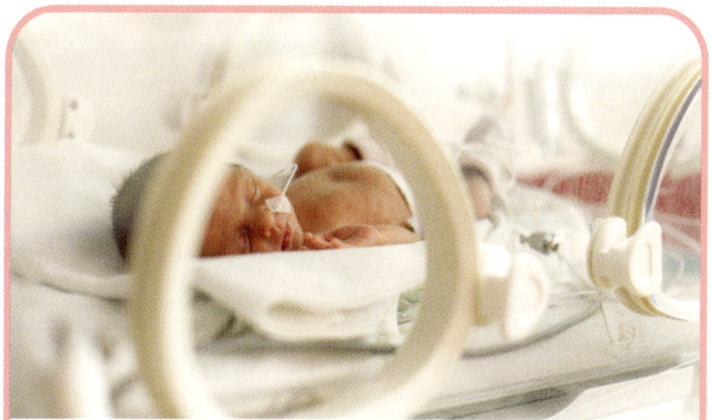

Born early

A premature baby is one that is born before the 37th week of pregnancy. Because they have been born early, they are at risk of health complications, so they are usually cared for in an incubator in a neonatal intensive care unit until they are healthy and strong enough to survive.

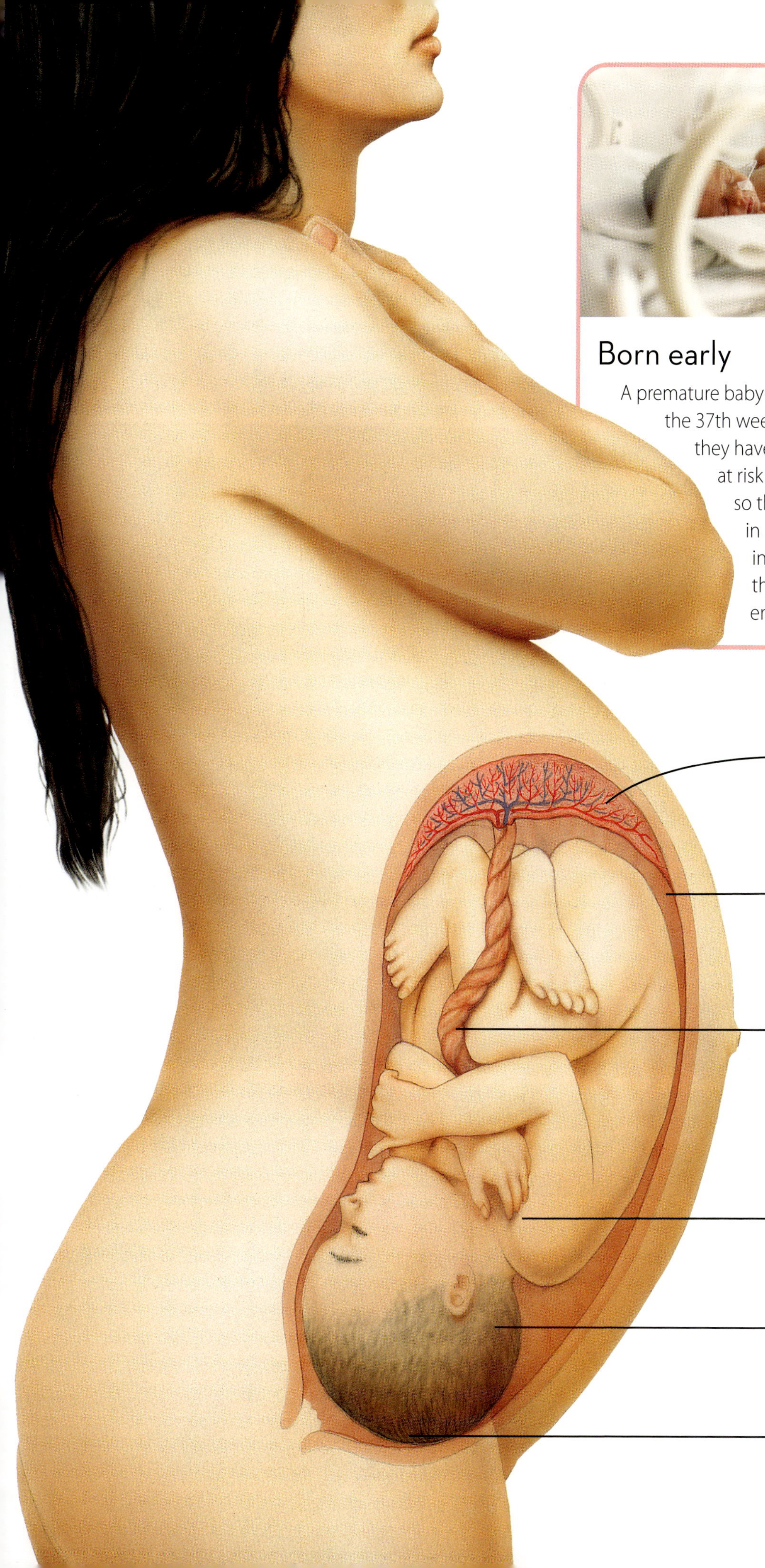

Fighting Germs

Millions of bacteria and viruses live on and in our body. These germs don't usually harm us because they cannot easily pass through our skin or the acid in our stomach. However, if they do get past these barriers, white cells protect us. Most white cells are contained in lymph tissue, such as the tonsils and spleen, as well as in our blood. There are several different types of white cells that make up the immune system. The most common are the polymorphs, which destroy germs. Sometimes, germs have protective coatings to help them avoid being attacked by polymorphs. When this happens, our bodies produce specially shaped structures called antibodies that lock into the germ's coating, breaking them apart.

Destroying a germ

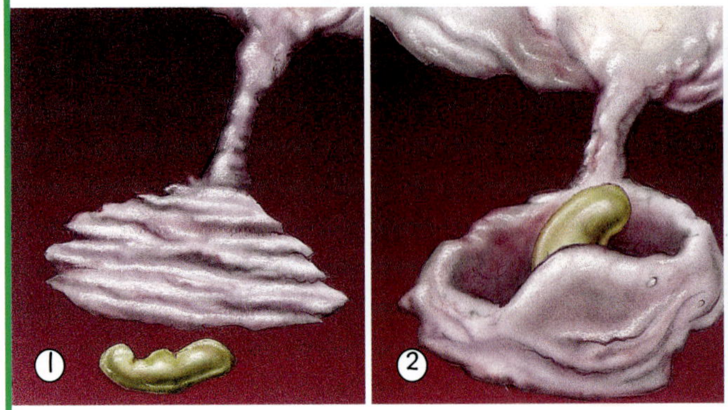

These pictures show how a polymorph white cell works. A chemical message alerts it to the presence of a harmful bacterium. The polymorph moves to where the bacterium is and makes part of its cell longer (**1**). This elongated part then surrounds the bacterium (**2**). Next, the polymorph cell membrane closes around the

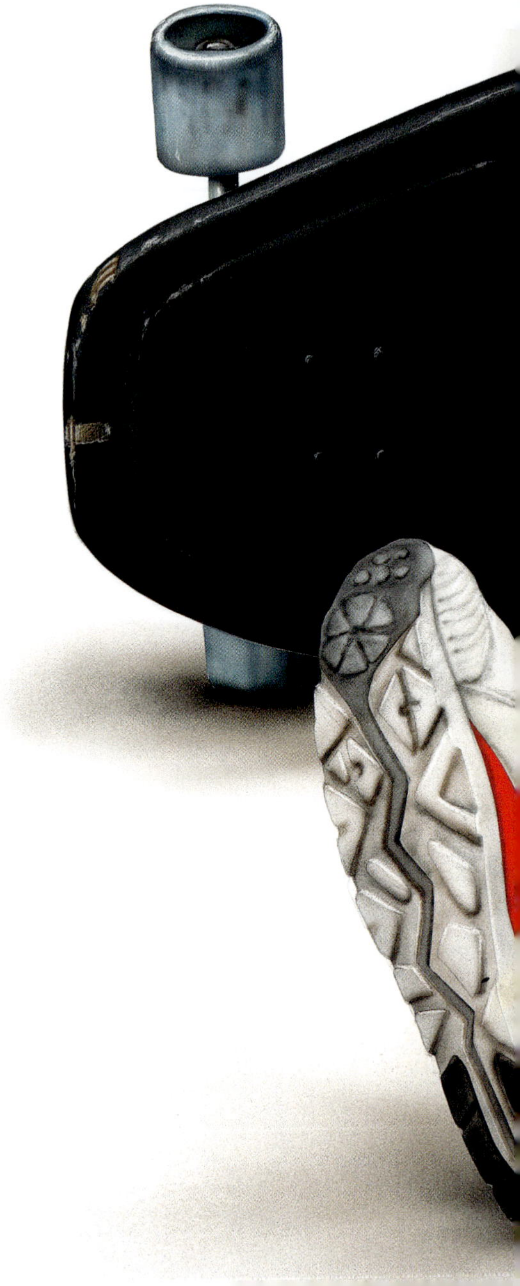

Immunization

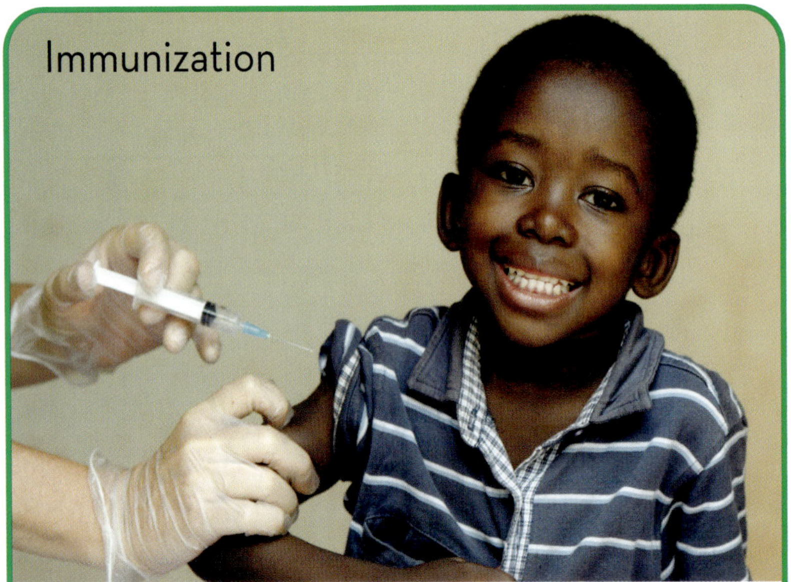

Many diseases that used to be very common are rare in developed countries today. This is because many people receive vaccines against these diseases, often when they are children, either by injection or by mouth.

Most vaccinations put dead or weakened germs into our bodies. These germs are not harmful enough to make us very ill, but they cause our immune system to produce antibodies that protect us from an attack by live, disease-causing germs. The biggest worldwide vaccination program ever began in 2020 to immunize against COVID-19 during a global pandemic.

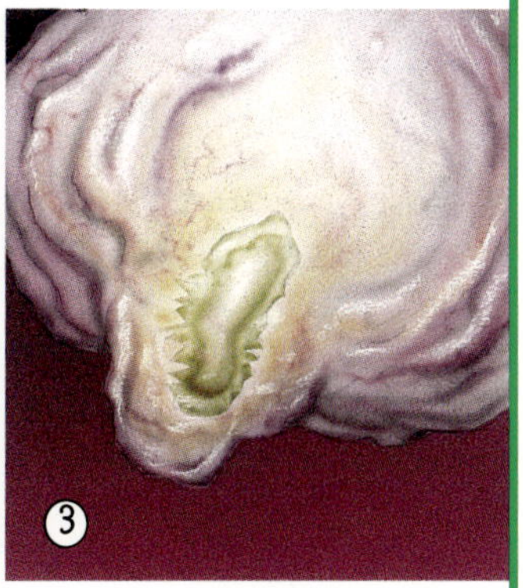

bacterium and chemicals are released by the cell to destroy it (**3**). Eventually, the polymorph moves on, leaving the bacterial remains behind.

White cells

If your skin is cut or grazed, its defense barrier is broken and bacteria can get in, causing an infection. Within a short time, chemicals released around the cut attract white cells from the blood. These cells are able to cover the germs and destroy them. Many white cells die in the process, and together with the germs they form yellow pus.

Spare Parts

Fortunately, today, many people with diseased or failing organs can be helped by transplants. The damaged organ – such as a heart or kidney – can be replaced by a surgically transplanted healthy one, if a suitable donor organ can be found. These operations rely on the goodwill of people who say their organs can be donated to others after they die.

Other people may be helped by artificial implants. For example, artificial prosthetic limbs have been developed for people who have lost a leg or an arm, or who were born without them. Surgeons can also use parts of the patient's own body to treat disease or injury. Veins from a patient's leg, for example, can be used to replace a damaged artery in their heart.

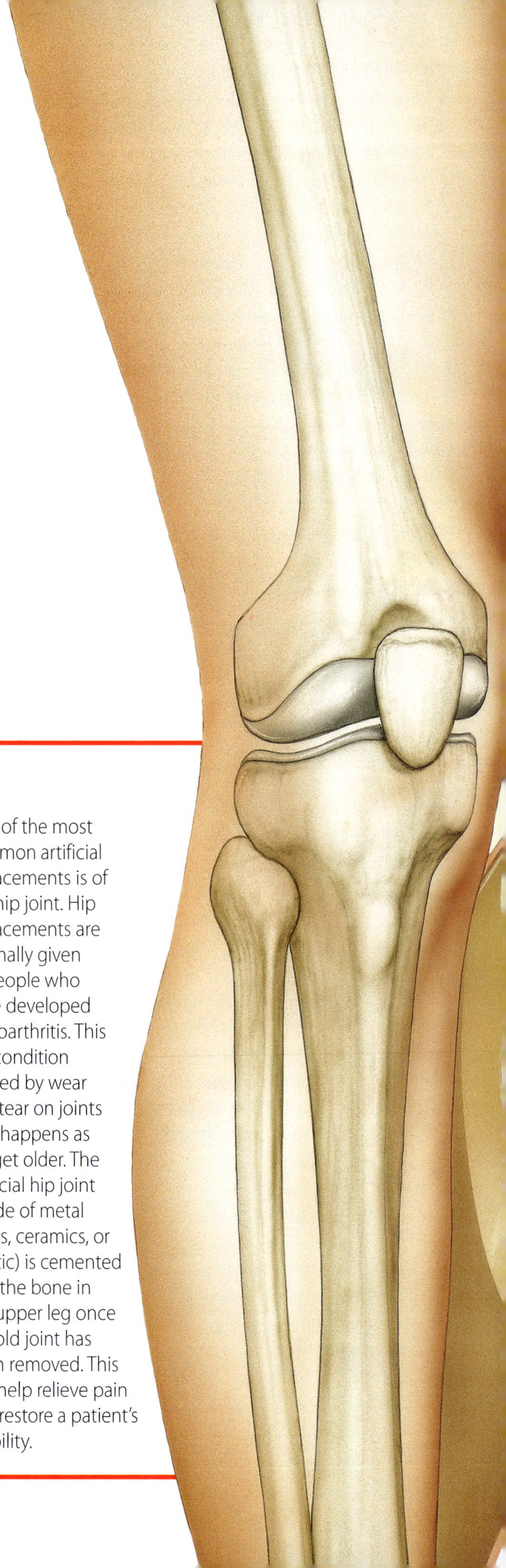

Joint replacements

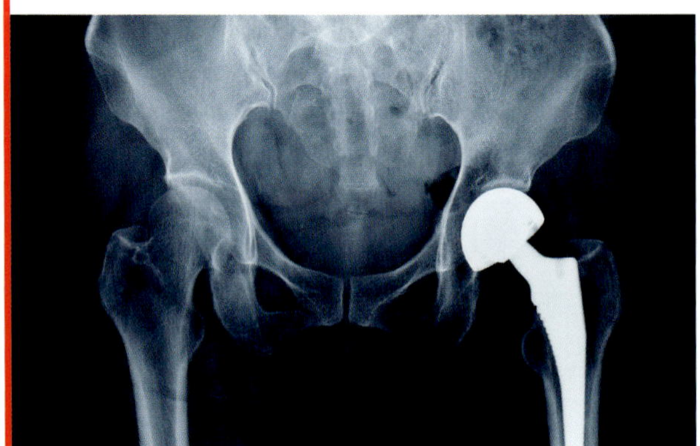

This X-ray (*above*) shows an artificial hip. Sometimes, replacement joints like this can set off metal detectors in airports!

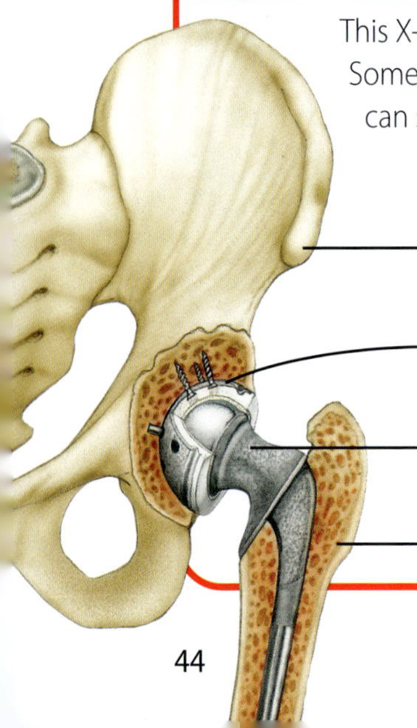

One of the most common artificial replacements is of the hip joint. Hip replacements are normally given to people who have developed osteoarthritis. This is a condition caused by wear and tear on joints that happens as we get older. The artificial hip joint (made of metal alloys, ceramics, or plastic) is cemented into the bone in the upper leg once the old joint has been removed. This can help relieve pain and restore a patient's mobility.

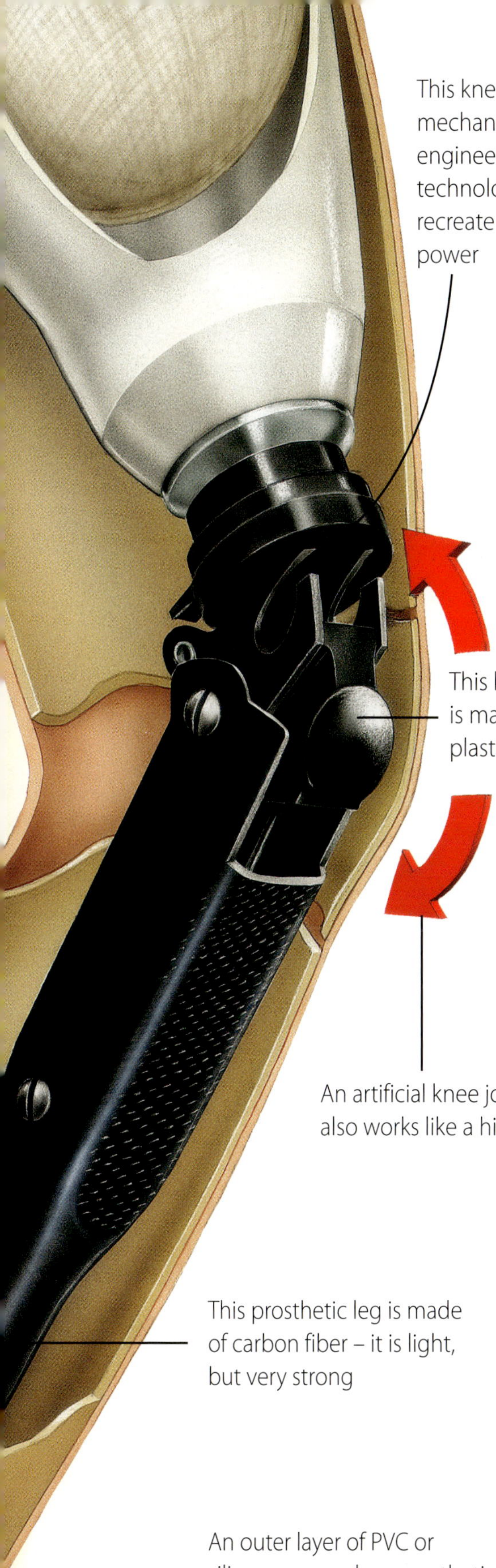

Coronary artery bypass

As we age, our arteries may become blocked with fat that has entered the bloodstream. If the coronary arteries become blocked, the heart may become starved of oxygen, and a heart attack may occur. By eating a balanced diet and exercising regularly, we can help to stop this from happening.

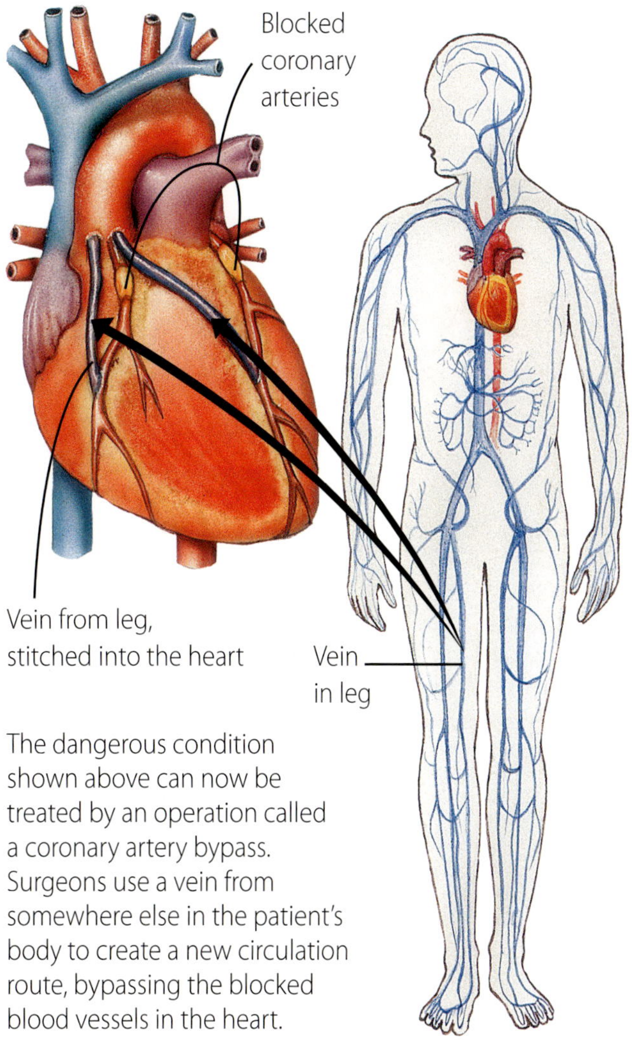

The dangerous condition shown above can now be treated by an operation called a coronary artery bypass. Surgeons use a vein from somewhere else in the patient's body to create a new circulation route, bypassing the blocked blood vessels in the heart.

Index